Tackling prison overcrowding

Build more prisons?
Sentence fewer offenders?

Edited by Mike Hough, Rob Allen and
Enver Solomon

KING'S
College
LONDON

University of London
International Centre
For Prison Studies

ICPR
Institute for Criminal Policy Research

CENTRE FOR CRIME
AND JUSTICE STUDIES

First published in Great Britain in 2008 by The Policy Press

The Policy Press
University of Bristol
Fourth Floor, Beacon House
Queen's Road
Bristol BS8 1QU
UK

Tel no +44 (0)117 331 4054
Fax no +44 (0)117 331 4093
E-mail tpp-info@bristol.ac.uk
www.policypress.org.uk

© The Policy Press 2008

ISBN 978 1 84742 110 4

British Library Cataloguing in Publication Data
A catalogue record for this report is available from the British Library.

Library of Congress Cataloging-in-Publication Data
A catalog record for this report has been requested.

Cover image courtesy of iStockphoto®
Cover design by Qube Design Associates, Bristol
Printed in Great Britain by Latimer Trend, Plymouth

Contents

List of figures and tables

Figures

Tables

Acknowledgements

We would like to thank all those who took part in the symposium recorded through this publication and in particular Phil Wheatley, Ruth Allan, Keir Hopley and their colleagues in the Ministry of Justice and the National Offender Management Service, and Sir Ken MacDonald for the spirit of openness with which they participated. We greatly value the fact that senior officials are prepared to engage in honest and robust debate with their critics on policy issues of such importance.

We are also very grateful to Siân Turner for her help in organising the symposium and to the Hadley Trust for funding the event.

Foreword

I write this foreword, not to endorse the views expressed in this publication, but to welcome an informed and critical debate of such an important issue.

In a mature democracy, what degree of risk the public will accept of further crime from known offenders and what sort of punishment is appropriate for offenders are properly for public discussion and are intensely political issues which our elected politicians have to grapple with and resolve. That debate is enhanced by good information, thoughtful analysis of it and expert opinion.

This series of papers provides a major contribution, mainly to that side of the debate which supports a reduction in the use of custody and an enhancement of interventions and punishments delivered in the community.

The end note highlights developments since the seminar, including changes to public opinion and media reaction to recent events. This challenging context partly explains the difficulty in delivering a major reduction in prison population. The public desire for increased protection from criminals and concern about violent crime and the threat of crime is part of the political reality and this cannot be ignored. Those who want to stem the apparently inexorable rise in the prison population have not only to present information and good analysis, but must find ways of making these changes acceptable to a public with a reducing tolerance level for crime and offenders.

As the Director General of the National Offender Management Service, I have to remain neutral in these difficult issues which, at an individual case level, are for the judiciary and, at a system level, for Parliament and the political process. I do, however, think that these papers will add much-needed information on and insight into these crucial issues.

Phil Wheatley
Director General of the National Offender Management Service
July 2008

Notes on contributors

Rob Allen is Director of the International Centre for Prison Studies at King's College London. He was previously Director of Rethinking Crime and Punishment at the Esmée Fairbairn Foundation in London, and before that, Director of Research and Development at Nacro, the crime reduction charity, and head of the Juvenile Offender Policy Unit in the UK Home Office. He has extensive experience of international penal reform work, mainly in the field of juveniles and alternatives to prison.

Carol Hedderman is Professor of Criminology at the University of Leicester and a member of the Griffins Society Council. She was formerly Assistant Director of the Home Office Research and Statistics Directorate. Her research interests include sentencing and sentencing effectiveness, the comparative effectiveness of different approaches to enforcing court penalties and 'what works' in prison and probation.

Mike Hough is Director of the Institute for Criminal Policy Research, King's College London. The institute carries out policy research for government and independent funders. He has published widely on topics including sentencing and attitudes to punishment, policing, drugs and anti-social behaviour. He was previously Director of the Criminal Policy Research Unit at South Bank University, and before that, Deputy Director of the Home Office Research and Planning Unit.

Jessica Jacobson is an independent consultant and Senior Visiting Research Fellow at the Institute for Criminal Policy Research, King's College London. She has conducted a number of studies into sentencing, and her publications include *The decision to imprison* (Prison Reform Trust, 2003) and *Mitigation* (Prison Reform Trust, 2007). She has also conducted research into public attitudes to sentencing and into policing.

Nicola Lacey is Professor of Criminal Law and Legal Theory at the London School of Economics and Political Science, having previously held posts at University College London, New College Oxford, and Birkbeck College, University of London. She is also Adjunct Professor at the Australian National University, Canberra and has been a visiting professor at New York University and at Yale. Her research interests range across criminal law, criminal justice studies, and legal and social theory. Her Paul Hamlyn lectures have just been published by the Cambridge University Press as *The prisoners' dilemma*.

Alison Liebling is Professor of Criminology and Criminal Justice at the University of Cambridge. She published her first book, *Suicides in prison*, in 1992 (Routledge). She has continued to conduct a wide range of empirical research in prisons, including key work on the impact of privatisation (*Privatizing prisons: Rhetoric and reality*, with A.

James, A. K. Bottomley and E. Clare, Sage Publications, 1997). Her most recent books are definitive works: *Prisons and their moral performance: A study of values, quality and prison life* (Clarendon Press, 2004) and *The effects of imprisonment* with Shadd Maruna (Willan Publishing, 2005).

Rod Morgan is Professor of Criminal Justice at the University of Bristol, a post he held prior to becoming HM Chief Inspector of Probation (2001–04) and Chairman of the Youth Justice Board for England and Wales (2004–07). He is also Visiting Professor at the London School of Economics and Political Science and at Cardiff University and a government-appointed adviser to the five criminal justice inspectorates for England and Wales. He has published extensively on crime, policing, prisons and punishment and is co-editor of the *Oxford Handbook of Criminology*.

Julian Roberts is Professor of Criminology at the Oxford Centre for Criminology. He was formerly Professor of Criminology and University Research Professor at the University of Ottawa in Canada. From 1992–2004 he served as editor of the Canadian *Journal of Criminology and Criminal Justice*. He is currently the editor of the *European Journal of Criminology*. He has published extensively on sentencing and on public attitudes to crime and punishment. He was a member of the Sentencing Commission Working Group.

Sanjiv Sachdev is a principal lecturer at Kingston University. He has previously worked as a research fellow at Cambridge University and as a trade union research officer at UNISON, the public service union, for eight years. His research interests focus on the employment relations implications of Public Private Partnerships and the Private Finance Initiative, especially in the criminal justice area, on the human resource management implications of corporate social responsibility and on issues relating to low pay. He has published widely in academic, think tank and trades union outlets.

Enver Solomon is Deputy Director at the the Centre for Crime and Justice Studies, King's College London and is the lead for the Centre's public affairs projects. He has previously worked as head of policy and research at the Revolving Doors Agency and as head of policy and communications at the Prison Reform Trust. He has published work on knife crime, youth justice, crime and the media, prison policy and sentencing. Prior to working on criminal justice policy he was a BBC journalist.

Introduction

Mike Hough and Enver Solomon

This book comprises the proceedings of a symposium held in May 2008 that examined government policy on prisons and sentencing. The event was organised by the three research centres in the School of Law at King's College London: the Centre for Crime and Justice Studies, the Institute of Criminal Policy Research and the International Centre for Prison Studies. It was funded by the Hadley Trust.

The symposium was organised to examine the latest proposals for prisons and sentencing set out in the government's review of prisons by Lord Carter published in December 2007 (Carter, 2007). The report put forward radical recommendations including the creation of a sentencing commission and the construction of large-scale 'Titan' prisons. It was felt by the three centres at King's College that these were significant proposals that needed to be subject to debate and independent critique. We therefore organised a symposium for senior criminal justice practitioners, policy officials, academics and voluntary sector staff. The intention was that the symposium presentations and discussions would feed into government deliberations on the proposals in the Carter Report.

Following publication of the report the government published two consultation papers. First, the Ministry of Justice set up a Sentencing Commission Working Group to consider options for a sentencing commission. The Working Group published a consultation paper on a 'structured sentencing framework and sentencing commission' inviting responses from interested parties (Sentencing Commission Working Group, 2008); thereafter it set out recommendations to the government, discussed in Chapter 4. Second, the Ministry of Justice published *Titan prisons* setting out detailed options for developing the model and seeking views on the proposals. Some of the authors in this volume have contributed to the consultations based on the presentations and discussions at the symposium. The most up-to-date position is set out in an endnote.

The event was held at King's College London and participants included the recently appointed Director General of the National Offender Management Service and former Director General of the Prison Service, Phil Wheatley, the Director of Public Prosecutions, Sir Ken MacDonald, the Chief Inspector of Prisons for England and Wales, Anne Owers, and officials from the Ministry of Justice and Treasury as well as academics and representations from criminal justice voluntary sector organisations.

We asked academic experts to prepare presentations to provide the basis for discussion at the event; and Professor Rod Morgan, who has served as Chair of the Youth Justice Board and HM Chief Inspector of Probation, summed up the proceedings by drawing out the main themes. This book brings together revised versions of the presentations together with this brief introduction, a chapter looking at future strategies, based on Rod Morgan's concluding comments at the seminar and an endnote bringing matters up to date.

The Carter reviews

Lord Carter's review of prisons published in December 2007, *Securing the future: Proposals for the efficient and sustainable use of custody in England and Wales*, is the second report on prisons and sentencing commissioned by the Labour government. Carter's first report was a wide-ranging review of the 'correctional services', that is, prison and probation, reporting to the Prime Minister, the Treasury and the Home Office. *Managing offenders, reducing crime: A new approach*, published in December 2003, was welcomed by ministers. Indeed the then Home Secretary, David Blunkett, described it as 'a once in a generation opportunity to reduce crime by radically transforming the prison and probation services' (Home Office, 2004, p 2). It led to the creation of the National Offender Management Service (NOMS).

At the time, political expectations for NOMS were high. Following publication, Home Office ministers said that the Carter recommendations, in tandem with the new sentencing provisions in the 2003 Criminal Justice Act, would mean that demand for prison places 'should match capacity and remain at a figure of less than 80,000' by 2009.[1] However, it quickly became clear that this was not going to happen. Prison numbers continued their relentless rise with the number serving new indeterminate sentences for public protection (IPPs) having a particularly inflationary impact. Ministers turned to Lord Carter once again for help, and four years after his second report he presented findings to the Prime Minister, the Treasury and the Secretary of State for Justice.

The latest Carter report is a considerable contrast from the previous one. The 2003 report provided an acute analysis of the pressures on the 'correctional services'. In particular the report gave proper weight to the political nature of the pressures on the correctional services:

> Behind [increasingly severe sentencing] there has been the interaction between public perception, media, politicians and sentencers. This interplay has helped to drive up the severity of sentencing. (Carter, 2003, p12)

Even if the detailed prescriptions for an integrated NOMS left much to be desired, the basic premise that the use of custody should be contained was welcome.

The 2007 report is much more bland. It treats as unproblematic the fact that there have been changes in public attitudes and in the climate of political life which have led to new and tougher sentencing provisions. It also presents the continued growth in the prison population misleadingly as a consequence of the government's success in increasing the number of offences brought to justice. One gets very little sense that the government's own policies and rhetoric have been significant drivers of the prisons crisis, unbalancing the equilibrium between demand and supply of prison places.

It is probably unrealistic to expect a document of this sort to offer a root-and-branch review of the government's penal policies, but as Carol Hedderman argues in her chapter, one might reasonably have expected the second Carter report on prisons to analyse why the recommendations in the first had failed so completely to deliver on their promises. After all, the first report suggested that it would achieve precisely what the second was asked to do. Instead, *Securing the future* takes a narrow view of the prisons problem – as something created largely by forces beyond the government's control, requiring immediate remedial action.

The report sets out proposals for an extensive prison-building programme on the assumption that doing so is unavoidable. There are three themes that underpin the report. First, that prison building on a substantial scale resulting in much larger custodial establishments is the only short-term solution to the current prison overcrowding crisis. Second, that in order to avoid a further crisis there needs to be more effective planning so that the supply of prison places meets the demand from the courts. This requires a more structured sentencing framework to ensure greater consistency and predictability. Third, the modernisation agenda for correctional services needs to be embedded further to deliver greater efficiency savings to operational management of the prison estate.

Where is the political context?

Perhaps the most striking feature about the most recent Carter report is its failure to recognise that at heart the problem of prison overcrowding is a *political* problem. Until 1992 none of the main political parties advocated the use of imprisonment as a solution to crime problems. From 1992 onward, the Labour Party started to mount a credible challenge to Tory credentials as the party of law and order, and the two parties became locked in a penal arms race, as is well described in Nicola Lacey's chapter in this volume.[2] As Labour became 'tough on crime' the Conservatives in turn discovered that 'prison works'. Penal parsimony turned into penal greed, as the main parties competed to 'out-tough' each other. The growth in sentencing severity charted by Carol Hedderman is not independent of this change in political climate, but a direct consequence of it.

A rational outcome – which many politicians will privately accept as the most desirable one – would be for the main political parties to establish a tri-lateral agreement to treat 'law and order' as off-limits in electioneering. This would entail self-denying ordinances against promising tough crackdowns on crime and on attacking the opposition for being soft on crime. However, other things being equal, politicians are unlikely to enter into such an agreement. Breaking trust and betraying such an agreement may yield a decisive electoral advantage.

Hence the key to solving the problem of prison overcrowding is, first and foremost, to find a political solution to this intrinsically political problem. Unless imaginative ways are found to help politicians find a resolution to their particular prisoners' dilemma, penal policy faces a dismal and costly future. The solution may need to be institutional, at least in part. Lacey suggests that some form of Royal Commission might serve to take the worst excesses of penal populism out of penal politics. In their chapter, Jacobson and colleagues argue that a permanent sentencing commission might serve much the same sort of function as a buffer between the political process and the courts.[3] The Carter Report argued for a sentencing commission, but one with a narrow remit that consisted of providing guidance to sentencers and statistical projections for government. If a commission is to be established, there is a strong case for ensuring that it has from the start a wide remit that includes informing and educating the media and the general public about the realities of sentencing practice.

Prison works?

In many ways the Carter Report can be seen as a return to the 'prison works' philosophy advanced by the last Conservative government. Although Labour has not explicitly made the case that prison works, the clear message from the Carter Report is that penal expansion is a necessary consequence of 'a concerted and successful effort to catch, convict and detain for longer periods the most dangerous and serious offenders' (Carter, 2007). Building more prisons is part of Labour's wider criminal justice agenda to bring more serious offences to justice and ensure that those found guilty receive tougher sentences.

There is a firm belief that once offenders are locked up, they can be rehabilitated. The report highlights apparent reductions in reconviction to demonstrate that the increased investment in prison-based interventions has had a positive impact. The fact that Labour has substantially increased investment in offending behaviour programmes, drug treatment and education and skills provision in custody demonstrates the extent to which ministers have been firmly committed to making prison work as a place of rehabilitation.

With the Ministry of Justice now embarking on a more ambitious programme of construction for large-scale prisons, the 'prison works' philosophy is taken even further. The Ministry of Justice's consultation paper boldly states that 'the case for Titans is a compelling one' (Ministry of Justice, 2008). There does not appear to be any doubt in the merits of large-scale penal expansion. Yet there are many gaps in the evidence the government is putting forward.

In Chapter 5 Alison Liebling draws on her research on the moral performance of prisons to argue that Titans run the risk of becoming unhealthy and damaging institutions. She presents research that demonstrates that smaller establishments tend to have regimes that treat inmates in a more humane and personal way. The government has argued that Titans could be designed as clusters of small, interlocked prisons. It remains to be seen whether this approach actually results in prisons that operate on a human scale.

In Chapter 3 Carol Hedderman also challenges the rationale for dramatically expanding the prison estate. Carter's analysis is neatly unpicked. She shows that reconviction rates have actually increased as the prison population has risen and that the rise in numbers has not been driven by bringing more offences to justice. Hedderman proposes developing 'a measure or "QALY" of public safety' to better demonstrate the cost and value of different interventions in order to reframe the public debate about punishment. Nor does one get a sense from the Carter Report that all the options have been fully considered. There is a significant body of experience in other jurisdictions about promising – and less than promising – approaches to containing prison populations, summarised in Chapter 7 by Julian Roberts.

'Modernisation' and efficiency savings

The drive for modernisation in the public sector has been pursued across government. The Prison Service has not been immune from this, facing regular pressure for efficiency savings, the introduction of key performance indicators, performance tables and competition from the private sector. In fact prisons have been at the forefront of privatisation in the UK since the first privately managed jail was opened in 1992.

The Carter vision is based on further modernisation to achieve greater efficiency in the operations of the prison estate. In particular, the Titan model is seen as a way of achieving long-term savings through economies of scale. The private sector is viewed by government as being best placed to deliver this. However, Sanjiv Sachdev raises several questions about the extent to which private providers have actually been a spur to innovation. The process of contestability clearly led to more flexibility within the public sector workforce. However, the economies achieved by the private sector appear to have been secured largely by the creation of a workforce that has worse pay and conditions than its public sector equivalent. Whether this is a situation that is sustainable in the long term remains unclear. The rapid turnover of the private sector workforce – and the tendency for employees to use private sector work as a stepping stone to the public sector – is a source of concern, as is the tendency of the private sector to cherry-pick senior public sector staff to fill top management positions.

Questions for the future

We wonder whether in hindsight 2008 will prove to be a turning point in the history of penal policy. To be pessimistic, it could emerge as that year when politicians lost all political will to curb the growth in imprisonment, and embraced the apparent inevitability of large-scale prison building. On the other hand, it is *just* possible that the opposite is true, and that 2008 will be seen as that critical moment when the government decided call a halt to the penal populism that has created the pressure for a near-doubling of our prison population over the space of 15 years.

At the time of writing the latter prospect looks more distant than the former – and more distant, too, than it did at the start of the Brown administration. That moment witnessed a brief rekindling of optimism about the return to a spin-free style of politics that was organised around principles of social justice. A year further on, we seem set for a period of febrile political competition in which 'law and order' will loom very large. We doubt that many politicians will be arguing the case for penal parsimony in the run-up to the next election.

Far-sighted politicians should be doing exactly this, however. In selecting our penal policies, we should take care to predict how crime might develop over the next two decades. What trends can we expect? Industrialised countries are now at the end of a period marked by exceptional economic stability. European and North American economies face recession, and are in any case likely to be challenged by the Chinese and South Asian ones. In a global economy which offers Britain only limited room for fiscal manoeuvre, the pressures will be to restrict wage increases and trim welfare expenditures. Other things being equal, we can expect a period of economic turbulence in which income disparities will grow. The poor are likely to get poorer, and crime is likely to rise. The 2007 Carter report was written against a backdrop of fairly stable crime rates, and very stable court workloads. It is worth thinking through the social and economic costs of mass incarceration in a period of steeply rising crime. If we do return to a period of rising crime, the penal policies that we currently pursue will most certainly look unsustainable.

Notes

[1] *Hansard*, House of Commons, written answers 19 April 2004. It was recognised that the population might increase in the intervening period.

[2] See also Ashworth and Hough (1996), Roberts et al (2003), Roberts and Hough (2005), Ryan (2003), Tonry (2004), Pratt (2006).

[3] See also Hough and Jacobson (2008) for a discussion of how a sentencing commission might be established.

References

Ashworth, A. and Hough, M. (1996) 'Sentencing and the climate of opinion', *Criminal Law Review*, November, pp 761–848.

Carter, P. (2003) *Managing offenders, reducing crime: A new approach*, London: Ministry of Justice.

Carter, P. (2007) *Securing the future: Proposals for the efficient and sustainable use of custody in England and Wales*, London: Ministry of Justice.

Home Office (2004) *Reducing crime, changing lives: The government's plans for transforming the management of offenders*, London: Home Office.

Hough, M. and Jacobson, J. (2008) *Creating a sentencing commission for England and Wales: An opportunity to address the prisons crisis*, London: Prison Reform Trust.

Ministry of Justice (2008) *Titan prisons consultation paper*, London: Ministry of Justice.

Pratt, J. (2006) *Penal populism*, London: Routledge.

Roberts, J.V., Stalans, L.S., Indermaur, D. and Hough, M. (2003) *Penal populism and public opinion: Findings from five countries*, New York: Oxford University Press.

Roberts, J.V. and Hough, M. (2005) *Understanding public attitudes to criminal justice*, Maidenhead: Open University Press.

Ryan, M. (2003) *Penal policy and political culture in England and Wales*, Winchester: Waterside Press.

Sentencing Commission Working Group (2008) *A structured sentencing framework and sentencing commission: A consultation paper*, London: Ministry of Justice.

Tonry, M. (2004) *Punishment and politics: Evidence and emulation in the making of English crime control policy*, Cullompton: Willan Publishing.

The prisoners' dilemma in England and Wales

2

Nicola Lacey[1]

> There [has] developed a war between the main political parties as a result of which the criminal justice system in general and prisons in particular have been the ultimate victims. One headline-grabbing change after another has followed, regardless of whether the system had sufficient resources properly to implement them. (Lord Woolf, reported in *The Guardian*, 17 March 2008)

Across the developed world today, we see striking contrasts in the level and quality of imprisonment. In 2006, imprisonment rates per 100,000 of the population ranged from about 36 in Iceland to a staggering 725 in the US. It is generally agreed that these differences cannot be explained in terms of crime rates, which – unlike levels of imprisonment – have risen and fallen over the last 50 years in broadly similar ways in most advanced democracies.[2] And while the humanity of prison conditions and the constructiveness of prison regimes cannot be so neatly assessed, there is plenty of evidence to suggest a similarly wide cross-national variation along these dimensions (see Whitman, 2003 ; Cavadino and Dignan, 2006).

In a recent book (Lacey, 2008), I argued that these variations in punishment can be explained in terms of a differentiated model of varying forms of capitalist economy and democracy. Individualistic 'liberal market economies' such as the US, the UK, Australia and New Zealand have, over the last 50 years, almost universally seen striking increases in the imprisonment rate, while 'coordinated' market economies such as those of northern Europe and Scandinavia have seen, by and large, much more stable levels of imprisonment.[3] In this country, we have experienced a rapid and continuing rise in punishment in the last 30 years (albeit that, happily, at 148 per 100,000 our imprisonment rate continues to be much nearer in scale to other European countries than to the US). In essence, I argue that the liberal market economies have found themselves in the grip of what we can loosely characterise as a 'prisoners' dilemma',[4] in which electoral arrangements and other institutional features of economic and political organisation have created a situation in which the strategic capacity for political and economic coordination necessary to reduce punishment is lacking.

In this paper, I focus on two specific questions. First, what can a comparative political economy analysis tell us about the purposes of imprisonment in this country? And second, what reform options does it suggest might be available to our politicians: Can the tide in this country towards ever greater imprisonment rates be reversed? Might it be possible to resist the tendency to use the prison system as a dumping ground for those in respect of whom more reintegrative social and economic policies have failed or are regarded as politically unfeasible? And could the political and economic dynamics feeding populist penal severity be more effectively countered? I will argue that a proper appreciation of the institutional structure underpinning the rise in punishment may help us to glimpse the beginnings of a solution, and that that solution may not be beyond the grasp of contemporary politicians.

The law and order arms race in contemporary Britain

The basic analysis of the rise of punishment in liberal market economies on which I am drawing is as follows. The disappearance of many secure jobs in the non- or low-skilled or manufacturing sectors after the collapse of Fordism led to the creation of a large minority of unemployed or insecurely employed people who were ungenerously protected by the social welfare system. Culturally included via the reach of state education and media technology, the economic exclusion of this large group, along with their sense of their own relative deprivation, fed both rising crime and a heightened sense of insecurity and demand for punishment among those securely employed.[5] In particular the support for strong law and order policies among a growing number of 'floating', median voters led to a situation in which criminal justice policy became highly politicised. In the context of this politicisation, within an adversarial, two-party political system, it became impossible for even the left of centre party, Labour, to sustain a focus on the social and economic causes of crime, along with a welfarist approach to responses to crime. Punishment has come to fulfil a set of relatively stable economic and political purposes: it is used to 'mop up' a segment of the population in relation to which other, more inclusive social policies in fields such as education and employment have failed; it serves to obscure that failure by displacing responsibility onto criminality; and it serves to underline government's credentials for taking effective policy action. As Downes and Morgan (2007) have shown, from the 1970s on, 'law and order' has become a salient electoral issue; and on Tony Blair's accession to the position of shadow Home Secretary, Labour began to abandon its traditional analysis in favour of a 'tough on crime, tough on the causes of crime' platform.

Newburn (2007),[6] building on Downes' and Morgan's analysis, has demonstrated that the really sharp upswing in imprisonment rates dates from this decisive moment. In his understandable quest to make Labour electable, Blair – like, as John Pratt (2006, p 174) has nicely put it, the sorcerer's apprentice – created a phenomenon whose dynamics were out of his control: as law and order swept into the flow of party political competition, both sides had little option but to strive to be the tougher on crime. Thus Blair as leader of the Labour Party and then Prime Minister, and successive Labour home secretaries, have put the emphasis firmly on the first part of the two-part equation. And though policies oriented to social inclusion – particularly in education, housing, social welfare and the introduction of the minimum wage – have formed an important object of Labour policy and have had some impact, it has been assumed that the stigmatising and exclusionary rhetoric and policy of the 'tough on crime' side of the criminal justice equation were entirely consistent with its inclusionary 'tough on the causes of crime' side (Machin and Hansen, 2003).

It is tempting to deplore the impact of this tough policy stance as a straightforward breach of the Blair government's vaunted commitment to defending both human rights and a more inclusive approach to citizenship. But it is important to acknowledge that the 'tough on crime' position had a clear place in the government's democratic agenda. The rights of citizenship were argued to bring with them responsibilities which were breached by crime. And the rights of offenders were constantly pointed out to be in need of adjustment to accommodate proper recognition of the rights of victims and potential victims – groups whose interests had often been marginalised in the tradition of penal welfarism. The Blair government accordingly defended its tough penal policy as evidence of its responsiveness and accountability to the needs of its citizens. As Peter Ramsay (2008) has convincingly argued, the package amounts to a distinctive and, if not attractive, entirely coherent approach to social citizenship – one based on the notion of individuals' responsibility to refrain from not only criminal conduct but also alarming others. This amounts in Ramsay's view to a conception of the need to protect 'vulnerable autonomy'; it finds its roots in 'new realist' criminology and one of its most vivid expressions in the anti-social behaviour order. Whatever the political recommendations of this vision, however, its costs in terms of traditional civil liberties are evident. We now live in a world in which it has become thinkable for the police to call for indefinite detention of terrorist suspects, and one in which the emerging national legal culture of human rights is being stifled less than a decade after its birth, abandoned or diluted wherever it threatens to pose constraints on criminal procedure in cases of serious crime.

The sad fact, moreover, is that the size and demographic structure of the prison population suggest that the socially exclusionary effects of the 'tough on crime' part of the criminal policy equation have, in relation to a significant group of the population, systematically undermined the inclusionary 'tough on the causes of crime' aspiration. The rate of imprisonment has continued to rise inexorably even in a world of declining crime, increasing by 60% since the inception of the downturn in crime in the mid-1990s.[7] Importantly for my argument, this increase in imprisonment was unplanned. The fact that it formed no part of the government's conscious strategy – notwithstanding the Home Office's own research unit's projections of the increase likely to result from prevailing policy (Councell and Simes, 2002) – is vividly and distressingly reflected in the inadequacy of prison capacity. This has become particularly evident in the last year, leading to incarceration in police cells and renewed plans for resort to detention on ships, reminiscent of the prison hulks which form one of the least attractive features of English penal history.

But where are politicians to turn for an escape from this counterproductive stalemate? Both the main parties are locked into a strategy of competition over the relative 'toughness' of their law and order policies; each is terrified of sustaining electoral defeats attendant on failing adequately to reassure the 'floating voter' of its determination to promote security by tackling crime as well as, increasingly, by acting pre-emptively through mechanisms such as anti-social behaviour or control orders, or mass surveillance by CCTV, to prevent it (Zedner, 2008). On 16 November 2007, the day after the Lord Chief Justice, Lord Phillips of Worth Matravers, made a public statement describing the shortage of prison spaces as 'critical' and as a direct consequence of ministers' failure to allow for the impact of their sentencing policies in planning prison capacity, the prison population stood at a record 81,547 (Carter, 2007, p 2).[8] Yet the huge social and economic costs of an ever increasing penal establishment seem to have disappeared from the landscape of political debate, and along with them any reasoned discussion of the real contribution of criminal punishment to reducing crime or improving public security.

The structure of this political prisoners' dilemma is not peculiar to Britain, but is rather a feature of adversarial, majoritarian political systems under contemporary economic conditions.[9] The focus on the supposed views of the median voter sets up a highly unstable and unsatisfactory dynamic in criminal justice policy making. There is, of course, much evidence about the complexity of public opinion on crime, demonstrating among other things a less punitive response to more contextualised questions about crime and punishment, and the extent to which public opinion may itself be led by political posturing.[10] Recent examples of the latter in the UK are, unfortunately, plentiful. For instance, the Ministry of Justice recently issued a press statement publicising an ICM survey whose results illustrated the complexity and context-dependence of public attitudes to punishment, while reflecting relatively strong support for community sentences and a concern with prevention through rehabilitation and reparation as well as deterrence. Jack Straw, the Lord Chancellor and Secretary of State for Justice, contributed a statement supporting 'rigorous effective community sentences'. Yet the press release went out under the emotive heading, 'Victims of crime want punishment'.[11] Even without this sort of political manipulation, the malleability of 'public opinion' makes it an unsound basis for policy development. To take just one example, recent empirical research in England and Wales found, within less than six months, the following apparently contradictory 'facts': first, that more than half those surveyed did not support an expansion of the prison estate and thought that government should find other means of punishment and deterrence; second, that 40% of those surveyed thought that sentencing was 'much too lenient', with a further 39% regarding sentences as 'too lenient'.[12] Yet notwithstanding such evidence of the ambivalence of 'public opinion', it seems that politicians' fears of the electoral costs of moderate criminal justice policy remain acute. In this context, the relative lack of insulation of criminal policy development from popular electoral discipline in adversarial, majoritarian systems, and the lack of faith in an independent professional bureaucracy are major problems (see Lacey, 2008, pp 72–5).

Yet this is not a tale of inevitability for liberal market economies. Canada, for example, has seen a relatively stable imprisonment rate over the last 20 years (Doob and Webster, 2006), and the Australian state of Victoria, while participating in the national trend towards higher imprisonment rates, has maintained its low level relative to other states within the federation (Freiberg, 1999; Cavadino and Dignan, 2006, p 84). In Canada's case, important factors seem to have included the checks and balances attendant on that country's distinctive federal structure; the influence of Francophone culture, particularly in the large province of Quebec; a relatively robust consensus orientation in politics; and a conscious sense of the desirability of differentiating Canadian politics and society from those of the US (Tonry, 2004). Victoria's historically low imprisonment rates – little more than half of those of its neighbour New South Wales over the last decade – have been bolstered, notwithstanding some increase in the 1990s, by state-level policies such as liberal use of the suspended sentence and the development of plentiful non-custodial sentencing options. But significantly – and less optimistically – given the extraordinarily high level of Aboriginal criminalisation in Australia, it may be that the modest Victorian levels of imprisonment have also been underpinned by the relatively low number of Aboriginal Australians in the state.[13] Our understanding of these differences is as yet relatively shallow, and a thorough analysis would need to look closely at the circumstances and institutional features of particular countries which either buck, or lead, the general trend towards penal harshness. An empirical study following up my analysis, in other words, would have to tackle the question of why it should be that the US and, to a somewhat lesser extent, Britain, most of Australia and New Zealand, are particularly strongly in the grip of the prisoners' dilemma of penal populism, notwithstanding their traditions of democratic freedoms and, hence, relatively robust histories of critical penal reformism.

Some aspects of the challenge facing these countries are, however, clear, even pending this larger and much-needed empirical analysis. One of them has to do with the structure of the public debate about penal reform. In a persuasive paper, Marc Mauer (2001) has analysed the pitfalls of the penal reform movement in the US. He argues that, in placing primary faith in attempts to demonstrate the high costs as compared with the benefits of mass imprisonment, reformers have failed to respond adequately to the strong emotional hold which images of retribution have on a populace which is further sensitised to the risks of violent crime by a TV media which propagates widespread images of both violence and effective policing in response to it. In a world in which both TV and printed media are increasingly in the hands of multi- or trans-national corporations, and in which the tradition of public service broadcasting is on the decline, the scope for national negotiation about moderation in crime reporting which so long characterised the Dutch, German and Nordic systems is rapidly becoming a thing of the past.[14] In this context, Mauer argues that 'reform efforts need to include broader constituencies', conveying 'an overarching vision of how to move from a punitive response to crime to a problem-solving orientation' such as that developed by the civil rights movement; 'expanding the discussion of crime policy beyond the day-to-day debates on the relationship between prison and crime to more fundamental concerns about the type of society we wish to create' and articulating 'a more positive vision of public safety' (Mauer, 2001, p 19). Mauer's call for an expanded public debate speaks to the informal sense in which electors as much as politicians are locked into what we might, loosely speaking, call a prisoners' dilemma: in voting for what they perceive as their self-interest, their individual preferences add up to support for a policy whose long-term consequences spell increasing social polarisation. And this, sadly, conduces to a mass incarceration policy: an effective penal apartheid for those surplus to economic requirements, and the need for ever more incapacitative penal policy not only in prisons but also in detention centres, through policing policies, surveillance such as CCTV, school exclusions and all the other features associated with the strategy of 'governing through crime' (Simon, 2007). Unmediated penal populism leads, in short, to a world for which perhaps few, even among the relatively advantaged, would consciously choose to vote.

Debating the costs of imprisonment

How, then, might governments in liberal market economies such as the UK help to generate a more expansive public debate about punishment? As the subtitle of the most recent report on imprisonment – 'Proposals for the efficient and sustainable use of custody in England and Wales' (Carter, 2007) – reminds us, public analysis tends to be as much preoccupied with economic efficiency as with victims' rights (as well as markedly more preoccupied with each of these than with fairness to offenders). This is hardly surprising given the salience of perceptions of economic competence to political credibility. But given that public money spent on criminal justice has a knock-on effect for resources available in areas such as health and education, there are reasons beyond purely economic ones for being concerned about the 30% increase in the proportion of GDP spent on 'public order and safety' between 1987 and 2005, or about the current £2.7 billion prison expansion programme.[15]

There is a substantial literature on the economics of mass imprisonment, much of it from the US. In a review of this literature, Marcellus Andrews (2003) has shown that, although on the most widely accepted calculations of the expected medium-term benefits in crime reduction of incapacitative imprisonment the net costs outweigh the benefits, the policy is nonetheless economically sustainable in the medium term. But sustainability is, of course, a different thing from optimal economic policy. Moreover, like criteria of macro-economic success, the way in which these economic calculations are made is highly contestable. In particular, the criminogenic effects of imprisonment, which decisively uncouples offenders from economic, family and social networks which could lead to reintegration, not to mention the damage to communities wrought by the mass imprisonment of certain groups, notably young black men, are inadequately acknowledged in many of these calculations. When we add in these social costs of mass imprisonment, the cost-benefit calculation looks fragile (see Pratt, 2006; Western, 2006). This contestability of the figures may confirm Mauer's view that too much faith has been placed in cost-benefit analysis. Yet it seems unrealistic to think that an expanded public debate about the future of punishment would not incorporate an attempt to analyse its utility, and wrong to think that it should not do so. Indeed, the lack of such a debate is one unfortunate side-effect of the emotional retributivism whose cultural power Mauer rightly recognises. This is a stance which has encouraged a kind of 'gut politics', which constructs harshness in punishment as an inalienable victims' right and which produces axiomatic claims, such as the then Home Secretary Michael Howard's infamous 'prison works', insulated from the flow of careful empirical investigation. And this genre of politics is, surely, precisely what needs to be avoided.

I would therefore argue that it is important to confront the question of the costs of imprisonment directly. A full analysis lies well beyond the scope of this paper, but a good starting point is Richard Freeman's (1996) classic account. Setting out from the stark question, 'Why do so many young American men commit crimes and what might we do about it?' Freeman offered an analysis of rising crime as fundamentally driven by the collapse of the unskilled labour market in the 1970s, producing a situation which presented people with low qualifications with bleak prospects in the legitimate economy. In this context, the rewards of crime became relatively more attractive, while the removal of offenders into the prison system produced a 'replacement effect', with other people – primarily young men, disproportionately African Americans – moving in to take up the opportunities vacated by those temporarily incapacitated by incarceration. What is more, Freeman suggests that more punitive sentencing may even have pushed up the price of illegitimate labour – or, to put it in another way, the rewards of crime – both by squeezing the supply of labour and by giving offenders strong incentives to maximise their own profits in order to discount the added risks of offending. While concluding from the existing research that levels of imprisonment prevailing at that time were economically sustainable, Freeman emphasised the fact that, as long as the illegitimate economy pays higher returns for a substantial group of workers than does the legitimate one, the level of punishment needed to produce a substantial deterrent effect or a substantial reduction of crime through incapacitation will be vast, and well beyond what would be politically acceptable even in the US.

Freeman's elegant analysis stands more than a decade after its publication as the most sophisticated and wide-ranging economic interpretation of crime in post-Fordist America. But I would argue that the upshot of his argument for penal policy is much more radical than his own solution implies. In essence – and in a relatively brief part of the article – Freeman advocated a compromise. He argued that it was necessary to develop skill-formation and labour market interventions to increase the legitimate rewards available to those who currently have a clear economic incentive to engage in criminal conduct. But in the political and economic context of late 20th-century America, he accepted that the way forward would have to include sticks as well as carrots: high levels of punishment as well as pre-emptive interventions to enhance legitimate opportunities for relatively unskilled young men.

In my view, Freeman here undersold his own argument. The implication of his analysis appears to be that the size of the prison population, *within politically conceivable parameters*, makes virtually no difference to the incidence of crime, which is fundamentally driven by factors outwith the criminal justice system. In a world in which – as Freeman acknowledges – it is the case both that high rates of imprisonment make at best a modest difference to crime levels and that politically feasible increases in the size of the prison system make either a marginal difference or possibly even have counter-productive effects, it seems sheer economic irresponsibility to invest an ever-growing proportion of GDP in the prison budget. In this country, it is high time for these arguments to be confronted directly by politicians and informed commentators. Given that governments' competence in managing the economy is key to their electability, even those of us who see the issue in terms other than the purely economic must surely acknowledge the importance of pressing home the message that increased prison spending is a form of fiscal mismanagement.

A further, baleful feature of the current public debate about the relative costs and benefits of punishment in the UK, as in several other liberal market economies, is its failure to set the social costs of crime in the context of the costs of other socially produced, and avoidable, harms. This point has been made forcefully by Hillyard and others in their development of so-called 'zemiology'.[16] This approach has focused on the costs of harms such as environmental and corporate harms, and on the impact of social policies such as welfare cuts on harms – including harms associated with criminal victimisation – which find their impact disproportionately among the least socially advantaged. Only once our public debate is mature enough to compare the relative costs of crime as conventionally defined and these broader harms will we be able to grasp the relative significance of punishment to social safety, and begin to assess rather than assume the relative contribution of punishment to the welfare of even victims of crime.

Taking the politics out of law and order: the bipartisan escape route

How are we to generate the sort of debate which is needed here? Clearly, it will not be an easy task. Happily, however, there is one major difference between the situation of political parties locked into the strategy of competitive penal populism in two-party majoritarian electoral systems and the prisoners' dilemma in game theory. This is that they are able to coordinate with one another. And this, surely, is where the beginnings of an escape from the cell of penal populism can be glimpsed. But this will only be possible if the two main political parties can reach a framework agreement about the removal of criminal justice policy – or at least of key aspects of policy, such as the size of the prison system – from party political debate. This might be done by setting up something akin to a Royal Commission, in an effort to generate an expanded debate which takes in not only the widest possible range of social groups but also a broad range of the non-penal policies and institutions on which criminal justice practices bear. In committing themselves to act on the outcome of such a commission, the two parties would distance the issue of crime control from the upward pressure created by electoral competition. More specifically focused institutional initiatives which provide a buffer between electorally driven political decision making and criminal justice decision making – sentencing commissions would be an obvious, and topical, example – would also be worth considering in the context of my analysis (see Jacobson, Roberts and Hough, this volume).[17]

But this would not be enough in itself to guarantee any success. A further important condition would be the reconstitution of some recognition of expertise in the field. It would be important not only to have any wide-ranging commission serviced by an expert bureaucracy but also, following implementation of its conclusions, to consign the development of particular aspects of future criminal justice policy to institutions such as sentencing commissions encompassing both wide representation and expertise. In other words, the distancing of criminal justice policy from party political competition would open up the possibility of the kind of solution to fiscal policy implemented through the Monetary Policy Committee (MPC) – a policy which is widely regarded as one of the key successes of the New Labour administration. By conferring the task of setting interest rates to an independent body of experts located in the Bank of England, making this body's deliberations transparent, and setting up robust mechanisms of accountability to parliament, Gordon Brown crafted a strategy which has commanded remarkable public and political support.

But is this strategy, which Brown developed as Chancellor, one which he should now, as Prime Minister, regard as broadly applicable to criminal justice policy? Significantly, both the bipartisan and expert orientation of my suggestion here are prefigured in his creation of cross-party task forces in a number of areas, including security, since his selection as leader of the Labour Party. The early signs, however, are not encouraging. Lord West, chair of the Security Task Force, said in introducing his first report that it did not propose lengthened periods of pre-charge detention for terrorist suspects because he had not seen a strong enough case for such a curtailment of civil liberties. The reaction from his political masters must have been swift. Within an hour, he was back on the news to tell listeners that he had misspoken.[18] Since then, the evidence that the Brown administration will follow the Blair track on law and order has accumulated, notably in the decision to extend the limit on pre-trial detention from 28 days – a period which is already significantly longer than that permitted in other comparable democracies (see Russell, 2007) – to 42 days. Most recently, in a move which underlines the 'prison as warehouse' mentality, we learn that the Prison Service, under pressure from government to deliver 'efficiency savings', is proposing to save £30m a year by keeping inmates in public sector prisons locked in their cells from Friday lunchtime to Monday morning, with all Friday afternoon education, skills training and offender management activities cut. One can hardly think of a policy more vividly in contradiction with any reintegrative aspiration.

The publication at the end of 2007 of Lord Carter's review of prisons[19] underlines the ambivalence of the messages emerging from the policy process. On the one hand, Lord Carter recommended that a working party be set up to consider the advantages of a sentencing commission, drawn broadly from the judiciary, legal profession and those with statistical expertise as well as victims' representatives, with the goal of producing the sort of structured sentencing practice which is thought to have helped to moderate imprisonment levels in Minnesota (and which receives sustained attention in another chapter of this book). He further acknowledged the need for an informed public debate about sentencing, proposed the restriction of indefinite sentences for public protection, and hinted at the desirability of effecting some degree of insulation of sentencing policy from the political process.[20] On the other hand, these recommendations were nested within a report whose main substantive proposal was to build a number of prisons so as to expand prison capacity by 6,500 by 2012. This is in addition to the current programme for an expansion of 8,500. Against this background, the more hopeful decision to consult on the establishment of a sentencing commission seems unlikely to have much impact. What is more, even if the report were to be implemented in full with the most exemplary efficiency, the prison population would, on the report's own calculations, and on the assumption that roughly the sentencing patterns predicted by the report continue, be set to exceed prison capacity again within a decade.[21] This is the case notwithstanding the fact that the report built in rather optimistic assumptions about the impact of its proposals on sentencing, and accordingly reduced its assessment of the likely prison population in 2014 from the Home Office's recent estimate of over 100,000 by 5,000 – a substantial (25%) adjustment to the projected increase.[22]

The idea of removing aspects of criminal policy from the arena of partisan competition along the lines of the MPC model which I have proposed may seem impossibly utopian. Why, after all, would politicians give up what has incontrovertibly become one of their favourite cards in the game of adversarial party politics? I would suggest, however, that it is entirely in their interests to do so. Under conditions in which both parties have unambiguously adopted a 'tough on crime' stance, neither has very much to gain from pushing it. The inevitable result is a highly reactive environment in which short-term policy development is the order of the day; in which the longer term effects and costs of criminal justice policy are far from the political agenda; and in which the interaction between criminal justice policy and other aspects of social and economic policy exist only in the rhetoric of 'joined-up policy making'.[23]

This is not, of course, to underestimate the challenge which the existing dynamics of law and order in this country pose for politicians. As I have argued, these are challenges which reach deep into the political-economic structure of the country. The main keys to unlocking the dynamic towards ever greater inequality, social and political conflict and criminalisation lie in a bipartisan approach at the political level and in interventions at the level of the labour market, education and training with a view to economic integration. The economic aspects of this challenge will not be met merely by creating a new tier of low-skilled and low-paid jobs which do not generate the kind of income or welfare support which allows those who hold them to feel fully members of the polity (see Young, 2003). And this, sadly, will be a tall order in Britain's political economy, whose competitive position has become increasingly dependent on low labour costs, low labour protections and job flexibility – implying a significant barrier to providing incentives to less skilled workers in the legitimate labour market capable of matching those in the illegitimate economy. The political dimension of the prisoners' dilemma may, in short, be easier to escape than its economic counterpart. But since the prisoners' dilemma implies our being locked into a policy scenario for which – properly informed about its long-term implications and able to coordinate decision making – it seems likely that a majority would not vote, an escape from its political dimension would in itself constitute an enrichment of democracy.

Notes

[1] This chapter draws heavily on material from Nicola Lacey, *The prisoners' dilemma* (2008), Chapter 4, 'Confronting the prisoners' dilemma: The room for policy manoeuvre in liberal market economies', and is reproduced with the kind permission of Cambridge University Press.

[2] See, for example, Newburn (2007, pp 433ff, 451–2).

[3] The 'liberal/coordinated market economy' distinction is drawn from Hall and Soskice (2001), pp 1–68.

[4] In the prisoners' dilemma in game theory, participants are unable to enter into an agreement: the upshot is that it is rational for them to choose, individually, a solution that is sub-optimal from each of their points of view (see also p 57, note 2, this volume).

[5] I am drawing here on Young (1999) and Garland (2001).

[6] On Blair's personal association with criminal justice policy, see also Newburn and Reiner (2007).

[7] This expansion in the imprisonment rate of England and Wales is yet higher than that of the US, which saw a 42% expansion during this period. England and Wales was, however, outdone by New Zealand, which expanded its imprisonment rate over the same period by no less than 68%: Carter, 2007, p 4. The increase in this country has been fed not only by policing and sentencing initiatives but by the creation of an estimated 3,000 new criminal offences between 1997 and 2006: see N. Morris, 'Blair's frenzied law-making', *The Independent*, 16 August 2006.

[8] Lord Phillips' remarks were reported in *The Times* on 16 November 2007.

[9] In Chapters 2 and 4 of *The prisoners' dilemma* (Lacey, 2008) I present an analysis of why most proportionally representative electoral systems work in a different way – and why, in New Zealand, the grafting of PR onto a pre-existing 'first past the post' system amid liberal market economic arrangements had markedly different effects from those which longstanding European and Nordic PR systems have had on penal policy.

[10] Beckett (1997), Chapter 1; Downes (2001) at p 67; Roberts and Hough (eds) (2002); Beckett and Sasson (2004); Hutton (2005); Brown (2006).

[11] Ministry of Justice, 16 November 2007.

[12] See, respectively, 'More prisons are not the answer to punishing criminals', www.guardian.co.uk/prisons/story/0,,2157364,00.htlm, 28 August 2007; Jansson et al (2007), Chapter 4.

[13] Gallagher (1995); Weatherburn et al (2003); Fisher (2007).

[14] As discussed in Downes (1989); see also Bondeson (2005, p 189); Cavadino and Dignan (2006, pp 108, 119); Pratt (2006, Chapters 3 and 6; 2008).

[15] The proportion of GDP spent on public order and safety rose from 1.8% in 1987–88 to 2.4% in 2005–06: HM Treasury (2007), Table 4.4, p 52. It appears that the projected cost of the prison-building programme *excludes* the cost of actually building the new prisons, which will be done through the government's private finance initiative: *The Guardian*, 17 December 2007, p 4.

[16] See in particular Hillyard and Tombs (2004, p 30); also Hillyard et al (2004).

[17] It has sometimes been argued that the structured sentencing implied by the move to guidelines issued by a sentencing commission leads to upward pressure on the prison population. However, there is evidence that this effect is felt primarily in relation to highly determinate systems such as the federal guidelines of the US, while more flexible systems have been associated with a decrease in resort to sentences of imprisonment: see T.B. Marvell (1995); K.R. Reitz (2005). I am grateful to Maximo Langer for alerting me to this research.

[18] *Today*, BBC Radio 4, 14 November 2007.

[19] Carter, 2007, Chapter 3; on the case for structured sentencing and a commission, see in particular paras 30–5; also Sentencing Commission Working Group Consultation (2008). For a pungent analysis of the proposal to expand prison capacity, see P. Toynbee, 'Posturing and peddling myths', *The Guardian*, 7 December 2007, p 41.

[20] Carter (2007, Chapter 3, paras 39(b) and 42-4). The Prison Commissions up to the early 1960s provided a precedent for an institutional mechanism, thereby ensuring a degree of political insulation for prison policy. I am grateful to Martin Wright for reminding me of this.

[21] As summarised in Carter (2007, Figure 3.1, p 29).

[22] Carter (2007, Figure 3.1 and Appendix G); for the Home Office estimates, see De Silva et al (2007).

[23] A notable feature of this environment is the selective way in which government draws on survey data. For example, a summer poll for *The Guardian*/ICM – 'More prisons are not the answer to punishing criminals' (www.guardian.co.uk/prisons/story/0,,2157364,00.htlm, 28 August 2007), reporting that 51% of those questioned 'think that the government should scrap its prison-building programme and ... find other ways to punish criminals and deter crime' – arguably opened up a real opportunity for a decisive political initiative on the part of the new government. Sadly, the opportunity was missed.

References

Andrews, M. (2003) 'Punishment, markets and the American model: An essay in a new American dilemma', in S. McConville (ed), *The use of punishment*, Cullompton: Willan Publishing, p 116.

Beckett, K. (1997) *Making crime pay: Law and order in contemporary American politics*, New York: Oxford University Press.

Beckett, K. and Sasson, T. (2004) *The politics of injustice: Crime and punishment in America* (2nd edn), Thousand Oaks, CA: Sage Publications.

Bondeson, U. (2005) 'Levels of punitiveness in Scandinavia', in J. Pratt et al (eds) *The new punitiveness*, Cullompton: Willan Publishing, p 189.

Brown, E.K. (2006) 'The dog that did not bark: Punitive social views and the professional middle classes', *Punishment and Society*, vol 8, p 287.

Carter, P. (2007) *Securing the future: Proposals for the efficient and sustainable use of custody in England and Wales*, London: Ministry of Justice, www.justice.gov.uk/docs/securing-the-future.pdf

Cavadino, M. and Dignan, J. (2006) *Penal systems: A comparative approach*, London: Sage Publications.

Councell, R. and Simes, J. (2002) *Projections of long-term trends in the prison population*, Home Office Statistical Bulletin 14/02, London: Home Office.

De Silva, N., Cowell, P., Chinegwundoh, V., Mason, T., Maresh, J. and Williiamson, K. (2007) *Prison population projections 2007–2014: England and Wales*, Ministry of Justice Statistical Bulletin, London: Ministry of Justice.

Doob, A. and Webster, C. (2006) 'Countering punitiveness: Understanding stability in Canada's imprisonment rate', *Law and Society Review*, vol 40, pp 325–68.

Downes, D. (1989) *Contrasts in tolerance*, Oxford: Oxford University Press.

Downes, D. (2001) 'The *macho* penal economy', *Punishment and Society*, vol 3, p 61.

Downes, D. and Morgan, R. (2007) 'No turning back: The politics of law and order into the millennium', in M. Maguire, R. Morgan and R. Reiner (eds) *The Oxford handbook of criminology* (4th edn), Oxford: Oxford University Press, p 201.

Fisher, G. (2007) *Victoria's prison population: 2001 to 2006*, Victoria: Victoria Sentencing Advisory Council.

Freeman, R. B. (1996) 'Why do so many young American men commit crimes and what might we do about it?', *Journal of Economic Perspectives*, vol 10, p 25.

Freiberg, A. (1999) 'Explaining increases in imprisonment rates', paper presented at the 3rd National Outlook Symposium on 'Crime in Australia: Mapping the Boundaries of Australia's Criminal Justice System', Australian Institute of Criminology.

Gallagher, P. (1995) 'Why does NSW have a higher imprisonment rate than Victoria?' *Contemporary Issues in Criminal Justice*, vol 23, Sydney: New South Wales Bureau of Crime Statistics and Research.

Garland, D. (2001) *The culture of control*, Oxford/New York: Oxford University Press.

Hall, P.A. and Soskice, D. (2001) 'An introduction to the varieties of capitalism', in P.A. Hall and D. Soskice (eds) *Varieties of capitalism*, Oxford: Oxford University Press, pp 1–68.

Hillyard, P. and Tombs, S. (2004) 'Towards a political economy of harm: states, corporations and the production of inequality', in P. Hillyard, C. Pantazis, S. Tombs and D. Gordon (eds) *Beyond criminology*, London: Pluto, p 30.

Hillyard, P., Pantazis, C., Tombs, S. and Gordon, D. (eds) (2004) *Beyond criminology*, London: Pluto.

HM Treasury (2007) *Public expenditure statistical analyses 2007*, Cm 7091, London: HM Treasury.

Hutton, N. (2005) 'Beyond populist punitiveness', *Punishment and Society*, vol 7, p 243.

Jacobson, J., Roberts, J. and Hough, M. (2008) 'A sentencing commission for England and Wales?' (this volume).

Jansson, K., Budd, S., Lovbakke, J., Moley, S. and Thorpe, K. (2007) *Attitudes, perceptions and risks of crime: Supplementary volume 1 to Crime in England and Wales 2006/7*, Home Office Statistical Bulletin 19/07, London: Home Office.

Lacey, N. (2008) *The prisoners' dilemma: Political economy and punishment in contemporary democracies*, Cambridge: Cambridge University Press.

Machin, S. and Hansen, K. (2003) 'Spatial crime patterns and the Introduction of the UK minimum wage', *Oxford Bulletin of Economics and Statistics*, vol 64, p 677.

Marvell, T.B. (1995) 'Sentencing guidelines and prison population growth', *Criminal Law and Criminology*, vol 85, p 696.

Mauer, M. (2001) 'The causes and consequences of prison growth in the USA', *Punishment and Society*, vol 3, p 9.

Newburn, T. (2007) '"Tough on crime": Penal policy in England and Wales', in M. Tonry (ed) *Crime and justice*, Volume 36, Chicago: University of Chicago Press, pp 425–70.

Newburn, T. and Reiner, R. (2007) 'Crime and penal policy', in A. Seldon (ed) *Blair's Britain 1997–2007*, Cambridge: Cambridge University Press, pp 318–40.

Pratt, J. (2006) *Penal populism*, London: Routledge.

Pratt, J. (2008) 'Scandinavian exceptionalism in an era of penal excess' Part I ('The nature and roots of Scandinavian exceptionalism') and Part II ('Does Scandinavian exceptionalism have a future?'), *British Journal of Criminology*, vol 48, pp 119–37, 275–92.

Ramsay, P. (2008) 'The theory of vulnerable autonomy and the legitimacy of the Civil Preventative Order', in B. McSherry, A. Norrie and S. Bronitt (eds) *Regulating deviance: The redirection of criminalisation and the futures of criminal law*, Oxford: Hart Publishing, pp 109–39.

Reitz, K.R. (2005) 'The new sentencing conundrum: Policy and constitutional law at cross-purposes', *Columbia Law Review*, vol 105, p 1082.

Roberts, J. and Hough, M. (eds) (2002) *Changing attitudes to punishment: Public opinion, crime and justice*, Cullompton: Willan Publishing.

Russell, J. (ed) (2007) *Charge or release: Terrorism pre-charge detention comparative law study*, London: Liberty.

Sentencing Commission Working Group Consultation (2008) *A structured sentencing framework and sentencing commission*, London: Ministry of Justice, www.judiciary. gov.uk/publications_media/general/sentencing_consultation310308.htm

Simon, J. (2007) *Governing through crime: How the war on crime transformed American democracy and created a culture of fear*, New York: Oxford University Press.

Tonry, M. (2004) 'Why aren't German penal policies harsher and imprisonment rates higher?' *German Law Journal*, vol 5, no 10, pp 1187–206.

Weatherburn, D., Lind, B. and Hua, J. (2003) 'Contact with the New South Wales court and prison systems: The influence of age, Indigenous status and gender', *Contemporary Issues in Criminal Justice*, vol 78, Sydney: New South Wales Bureau of Crime Statistics and Research.

Western, B. (2006) *Punishment and inequality in America*, New York: Russell Sage Foundation.

Whitman, J.Q. (2003) *Harsh justice*, Oxford: Oxford University Press.

Young, J. (1999) *The exclusive society*, London: Sage Publications.

Young, J. (2003) 'To these wet and windy shores: Recent immigration policy in the UK', *Punishment and Society*, vol 5, p 449.

Zedner, L. (2008) 'Fixing the future: The pre-emptive turn in criminal justice', in B. McSherry, A. Norrie and S. Bronitt (eds), *Regulating deviance: The redirection of criminalisation and the futures of criminal law*, Oxford: Hart Publishing, pp 35–58.

Building on sand: why expanding the prison estate is not the way to 'secure the future'

3

Carol Hedderman

> There are lots of nice things you can do with sand; but do not try building a house on it. (C.S. Lewis, 1943)

Over the last decade the prison population has grown from 65,300 to 83,200.[1] In the next decade the demand for prison places in England and Wales will outstrip the number planned. Others have, and will, debate the important questions this raises about the role prison plays in society, including whether we should use prison at all (see Walker, 1991; Hudson, 2003). This chapter, however, adopts a purely utilitarian view point. From this perspective, there seem to be only two solutions to a position in which the demand for prison places exceeds supply: build faster or change the way custodial sentences are used. The government has chosen to focus on the first option because this appears to be the only approach which avoids two political elephant traps: being portrayed as soft on crime; and, simultaneously, interfering with judicial independence.

This is the course this government – and the preceding Conservative administration[2] – has been pursuing for as long as the prison population has been rising, so it would be unfair to claim that the report of an investigation led by Lord Patrick Carter (2007) persuaded the government to take it. However, Carter's report does reassure the government that it is feasible to physically build a way out of the problem, by confirming that the greater use of imprisonment has been associated with more offenders being brought to justice and reduced reconviction; and by asserting that, anyway, this is what the public want. A reexamination of the evidence on which these conclusions are based suggests that this reassurance is false comfort.

In this paper it will be argued that, contrary to Carter's claims, the increased use of imprisonment has not been driven by more offences being brought to justice; that prison reconviction rates have escalated as the population has increased; and that the public appetite for prison is more limited and more susceptible to reasoned argument than Carter acknowledges. Finally, it is argued that expanding the prison estate will generate, not satiate, demand.

A tale of two Carters

In 2003, Lord Carter of Coles presented a report on 'managing offenders, to reduce crime and maintain public confidence' (Carter, 2003, p 4). This report explained why the prison population had grown to unprecedented levels and what should be done about it. The main explanation put forward for the increase in the sentenced population was that sentencers were responding more severely to the cases before them, although these had neither become more serious nor more numerous. Carter's solutions at that time involved reserving custody for dangerous and serious offenders; making non-custodial penalties more attractive to sentencers; and making the transition from custody to community seamless by bringing the Prison and Probation Services together in one new organisation – the National Offender Management Service (NOMS). It was anticipated that the new service and extra community orders would be paid for by the saving in prison places.[3]

Despite the fact that the government immediately accepted most of Carter's (2003) conclusions, the prison population has continued to grow to a point where emergency measures have been used to contain and manage it through the use of police cells and early release. As the plans relied on making the use of non-custodial options more flexible and persuading sentencers that these were alternatives to custody, some commentators predicted that the prison population would continue to rise. Hedderman (2006), for example, argued that this was virtually inevitable. Four of the reasons for this are worth reiterating. First, sentencers consistently say there is no real substitute for custody, remaining convinced that they are using it as a last resort. Second, the history of introducing new options as 'alternatives to custody' (for example, community service and combination orders) is that such sentences quickly become alternatives to each other and go down tariff. Third, the prison population was rising because of recalls as well as sentencing; and the breach provisions of the 2003 Criminal Justice Act were bound to increase the numbers going to prison by the back door rather than directly because of a sentencing decision. Fourth, non-statutory sentencing guidelines have a record of being ineffective so the chances that the purely advisory Sentencing Guidelines Council would significantly alter sentencing behaviour were slim.

The most obvious contrast between Carter's 2003 and 2007 reports is that while the former analysed the reasons for the rise in the sentenced population and suggested how it might be slowed if not reversed, the latter makes a number of additional but largely un-evidenced assertions about the reasons for the increase and focuses on how to cope with further rises in demand. It is also rather odd that the few additional analyses which are included in the 2007 report all relate to a 10-year period beginning in 1995 – two years after the increase began and after the prison population had already risen by 6,410 (from a low of 44,552 in 1993) (Home Office, 2001).

A second point to note about the 2007 report is that there is no direct discussion of why the measures Carter proposed in 2003 have not limited the prison population in the ways he anticipated. Indeed, according to Carter (2007, p 14), it is the National Audit Office which expected those changes to limit the prison population to 80,000 by 2008. But surely the reader has a right to know that the man in charge of the current review recommended most of the recent changes which were expected to limit the growth in prisoner numbers and that those changes have not had the effects he anticipated?

The lack of such a declaration of interest raises questions about whether Lord Carter's role in creating the current context has affected his explanation for the increase. Certainly, this account has undergone considerable revision over the last four years with pre-eminence now being given in the report's covering letter to the Prime Minister to 'a concerted and successful effort to catch, convict and detain for longer periods the most dangerous and serious offenders'. The courts' use of custodial sentences for low-risk offenders is acknowledged to be problematic but this factor is now accorded a subsidiary rather than a leading role. For this reason, solutions which might reverse this trend, such as a structured sentencing framework and a permanent sentencing commission, are treated as being worthwhile in the long term rather than urgently required. Because a core element of Carter's preferred explanation is that the prison population is rising because the numbers being caught and convicted for serious offences are growing, the new preferred solutions are to expand the prison estate by 6,500 places within five years, with larger individual prisons providing most of the increased capacity. Not only are these 'Titans' to offer better value for money, but Carter also advises the Prime Minister that they will provide 'much improved chances of reducing reoffending and crime'. No evidence is provided to support this claim. This is particularly troubling given that both the Chief Inspector of Prisons and those with direct experience of operating the French equivalent of Titans have strong reservations about their effectiveness (*File on Four*, BBC Radio 4, 18 March 2008).[4]

The drivers of the prison population

Regardless of whether one accepts the conclusion drawn in *Managing offenders, reducing crime* (Carter, 2003), it is hard to fault the underlying analyses about why the prison population has doubled since the early 1990s. Criminal justice legislation over the last decade has been characterised by increasing the penalties for a wide range of existing offences and expanding the range of criminal offences. The number remanded after conviction but before sentence has risen sharply. More people are being sentenced to custody for very short periods of time. Meanwhile the prison sentences imposed for some serious offences have increased dramatically, particularly in terms of their length. The chances of prisoners getting out early have been reduced as the Parole Board and prison governors have become increasingly risk-averse following a small number of high-profile cases in which those released have offended seriously. The scope for criminal justice officials to deal informally or leniently with minor infractions of community orders or post-release licences has been limited by statute and by increasingly restrictive operational guidance, regardless of whether the infraction involved further offending. In other words, the prison 'sink' is filling up because the flow from the courts has been increased and the flow out through parole and early release has been reduced. Moreover, more of those who do come out are being poured back in and at a faster rate. Additionally, since Carter's analysis was published, judges have been empowered to impose new indeterminate sentence of Imprisonment (or Detention) for Public Protection (IPP). The fact that 1,450 of these were imposed in the full first year of operation (RDS NOMS, 2007b) suggests they have taken up this power with alacrity. As Carter (2007) acknowledges, this is happening in a context in which crime has decreased, although he does not repeat his 2003 conclusion that the increased use of custody had made only a modest contribution to the fall in crime.

In *Securing the future*, Carter (2007) gives prominence to three additional factors which have contributed to the rise in the prison population: the impact of more offenders being 'brought to justice'; the effectiveness of imprisonment in reducing reoffending; and public attitudes. His presentation of evidence in relation to these factors is inadequate and, it is argued, highly misleading.

The impact of more offenders being brought to justice

> Whilst these volume crimes have reduced significantly, *the number of offenders sentenced in all courts has increased, from 1,354,294 in 1995 to 1,420,571 in 2006, an increase of 5% (see Figure 1.2)*. The number of offenders sentenced in all courts peaked at 1,547,353 in 2004, an increase of 14%, since 1995. This reflects the government's priority to reduce crime and increase the number of offences brought to justice. (Carter, 2007, p 5, emphasis in original)

This quotation comes from a section of the Carter Report headed 'Drivers of the prison population', so, despite the careful drafting, the intended implication is clearly that the number of offenders being sentenced is one such driver. It is possible to reach this conclusion only if one focuses on the period 1995 to 2005. The logical starting point for a genuinely independent assessment is when, or just before, the prison population began to rise. Adopting the latter approach shows that the numbers being sentenced fell successively from 1987 to 1995 and that the numbers being sentenced in the succeeding years did not reach pre-1995 levels again until 2003 (see Figure 3.1).

The most obvious conclusion to draw from Figure 3.1 is that the rise in the prison population bears little relation to the overall number being sentenced. Indeed the rise began at the very point the numbers being sentenced were declining most sharply; and the prison population is continuing to increase despite a recent dip in sentenced numbers.

Figure 3.1: The prison population and total numbers sentenced

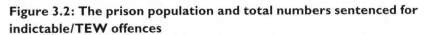

Source: Based on figures from Home Office (2003), RDS NOMS (2005, 2006, 2007a, 2007b) and Prison Service (2006, 2007, 2008)

The lack of connection between the prison population and total numbers sentenced is not surprising given that most court cases involve comparatively trivial summary offences. It is more reasonable to expect the prison population to increase if the number of more serious (indictable and triable-either-way (TEW)) cases rises. However, Figure 3.2 shows that the number of serious cases being sentenced has been relatively static throughout most of the period in which the prison population has grown, and has actually been declining since 2003.

Figure 3.2: The prison population and total numbers sentenced for indictable/TEW offences

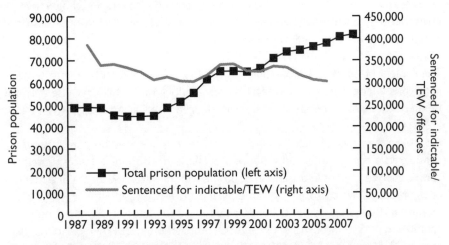

Source: Based on figures from Home Office (2003), RDS NOMS (2005, 2006, 2007a, 2007b) and Prison Service (2006, 2007, 2008)

While the overall numbers being sentenced for all offences and the numbers sentenced for indictable/TEW offences are not driving the prison population up, it is true, as Carter (2007, p 7) claims, that 'the proportion of different types of serious offences coming before the courts has changed with violence against the person, robbery and drug offences increasing at the expense of burglary and theft offences' (assuming that 'coming before the courts' means sentenced). This, together with his tentatively expressed view that this has resulted in a '... perhaps more serious, offence mix' (p 7), suggests that the numbers going to prison have increased because the courts are dealing with more serious cases. The fact that the numbers sentenced for violent offences rose by 40% between 1995 and 2005, while the numbers sentenced to custody rose by 53%, could be interpreted as evidence that the violent cases coming to court now are more serious than they were a decade ago. However, using average sentence length as a crude indicator of seriousness suggests that this is not the case: average sentence length has fluctuated between 16 and 19 months over the entire period. For drugs, the numbers sentenced to custody rose by 47% over the same period but this conceals a very mixed underlying picture in which the numbers sentenced for drug offences peaked in 1999, fell in 2000 and 2001, peaked again in 2003 and fell again in 2004 and 2005. The use of custody for such cases rose slightly over the period, from 17% to 20% (with reductions in 2002 and 2003). Using sentence length as a measure of case seriousness shows that the average did not rise above 30 months until 2001 and has since fluctuated between 34 and 37 months. None of these figures support a simple explanation couched in terms of the courts responding to a significantly larger or more serious caseload.

Of course, even when relatively static, the long sentences imposed for serious offences make a large contribution to the prison population. In fact, it is because sentence length plays such an important part in determining the size of the prison population that Carter's comments about offences brought to justice being an important driver of it are essentially a red herring. To see this, it is worth looking at the relationship between the number of serious offences being sentenced to custody and the overall use of custody each year (Figure 3.3a). This shows just how few of the custodial sentences imposed each year relate to serious offences.

The sentencing of these serious offences has made a large contribution to the rise in the prison population, mainly because they are long rather than because they are frequent – a point Carter previously acknowledged (see Carter, 2003).

Although not included in Carter's list of 'more serious' offences, burglary is generally considered a serious offence by the public. Like other serious offences, burglary's contribution to the rise in the prison population lies mainly in the length of sentences being imposed, which rose from an annual average of 12 months in 1995 to 17 months in 2005. The number of burglars sentenced to custody remained at between 12,000 and 14,500 throughout 1995–2005, although the overall number of burglars sentenced dropped from 35,450 in 1995 to 22,652 in 2005. While these figures show that the courts are dealing more severely with the burglars who do reach

Figure 3.3a Changes in the overall use of custody and the use of custody for serious indictable offences 1995–2006

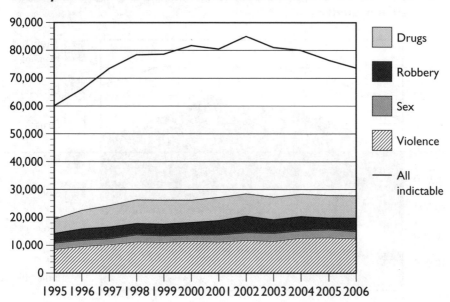

Source: Based on figures from Home Office (2003), RDS NOMS (2005, 2006, 2007a, 2007b) and Prison Service (2006, 2007, 2008)

court, as the number of burglars being sentenced has dropped over this period by an average of 1,400 per year, it is hard to construe this as evidence of the government's commitment to bringing more offences to justice.

The largest numeric and proportionate increases in the sentencing of individual indictable offences occurred in relation to theft and handling. The numbers sentenced to custody rose by nearly a third (from 15,637 in 1995 to 20,472 in 2005) even though the overall number sentenced by the courts for these offences declined from 116,078 to 103,318 (RDS NOMS, 2007b). Figure 3.3b shows that this change in sentencing behaviour has played an important part in the rise in the numbers received into prison.

Given that the average length of sentences imposed for theft and handling has dropped from 6.3 to 4.3 months over the same period, it could even be true that those going to prison for these offences may actually have committed *less* serious offences than those sentenced to custody 10 years earlier. Of course these cases do not add very much to the prison population because they involve such short sentences, but they do add very significantly to prison receptions and the costs of imprisonment. The consequences of this change in sentencing behaviour is particularly marked in relation to the female prison population because this is the offence for which most women are sentenced and a higher proportion of the female prison population are sentenced to short periods of imprisonment (Hedderman, 2004).

Figure 3.3b Changes in the overall use of custody and the use of custody for serious indictable offences 1995–2006: adding in burglary and theft and handling

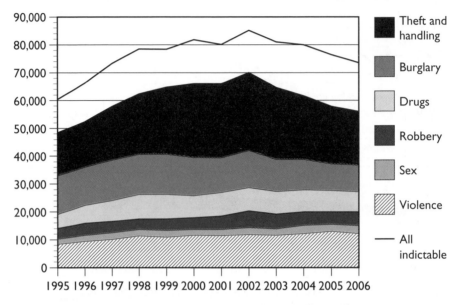

Source: Based on figures from Home Office (2003), RDS NOMS (2005, 2006, 2007a, 2007b) and Prison Service (2006, 2007, 2008)

Two other groups of offences have seen sharp increases in the numbers and proportions sentenced to custody between the mid-1990s and mid-2000s. The numbers sentenced for indictable and summary 'other non-motoring' offences[5] rose by about 25% over this period, but the proportion being sentenced to custody rose by 82% in the case of 'other non-motoring' indictable offences and by 102% in the case of 'other non-motoring' summary offences. This equates to between 11,000 and 12,000 more offenders being sent to prison for such offences in 2006 than 1995. As with theft and handling, average sentence length has been static in both cases (at 9 and 2.8 months, respectively), indicating little change in offence seriousness.

It is hard to see on the basis of these analyses how Carter could conclude that the rise in the prison population is a consequence of successfully bringing more offences to justice except in the sense that it is recycling the 'usual suspects' more quickly. This is the predictable – and possibly even intended – consequence of a government PSA[6] target framed in terms of bringing *more offences*, rather than *more offenders*, to justice. This would explain why sentencing statistics (RDS NOMS, 2007a) show that the proportion of offenders with 10 or more previous convictions coming to court for sentencing is increasing, while the proportion of first-time offenders coming to court is stable.[7] In other words, it may be causing the 'usual suspects' to develop longer records, without bringing additional offenders into the net. Given that this pattern is particularly evident at the magistrates' court level, this may help to explain why individuals convicted of comparatively minor offences are now more likely to be given custodial sentences. This may be what the government intended but it is less clear that this is what the public want.

The link between the greater use of custody and reconviction

> Overall proven re-offending has reduced by 5.8% comparing 2000 to 2004 using a predicted rate, with re-offending by former prisoners reducing by 4.6% on the same basis. This reflects the increased investment in offender interventions both in prison and the community. (Carter, 2007, p 5)

It has been well established that reconviction rates following different sentences vary largely because of differences in the types of offenders who are given such sentences. Studies conducted on samples taken from those sentenced to community penalties or released from prison in the early 1990s show that once allowance was made for differences in offending and sentencing history, age and sex, reconviction rates for the most commonly used forms of community supervision and imprisonment varied by only a percentage point or two, whereas there were large differences in the 'raw' rates (see Lloyd et al, 1994; Kershaw and Renshaw, 1997). This is why, when reconviction results are used to compare the impact of prison and probation, statistical modelling is conducted to remove the effect of differences in the case mix each service is required to supervise. This is also done to assess changes in their effectiveness over time.

Recently, analyses of 'modelled' data have been used to claim that the effectiveness with which the prison and probation services supervise offenders is improving (see Spicer and Glicksman, 2004, for example). While the causes of the change cannot be known for certain, it is reasonable to assume that better supervision has played a part in the fall in reconviction these analyses demonstrate (Hedderman, 2006). However, these modelled reconviction rates should not be used when assessing the impact of sentencing behaviour, as the effects they strip out include changes in the apparent characteristics of offenders which may be a consequence, rather than a cause, of changes in sentencing behaviour. Evidence for this view lies in Carter's 2003 analysis and more recent statistics (RDS NOMS 2007a)[8] which confirm that, since the rise in the prison population began, offence seriousness has remained stable or fallen, the proportion of first time offenders being sentenced has been stable but the proportion sentenced to custody has risen, and the proportion of those convicted who have high numbers of previous convictions only began to rise in 2002 (well after the rise in the prison population began).

Although they are a poor measure of the work of the prison and probation services, currently raw reconviction rates are the best available measure for assessing the impact of changes in sentencing behaviour. These show that Carter's (2007, p 5) claim, based on modelled reconviction rates, that there have been 'reductions in re-offending', is both untrue and misleading. There has been a reduction in the modelled 2004 reconviction rate compared with 2000, but raw reconviction rates published in the annexes of the latest reducing reoffending PSA report (Cunliffe and Shepherd, 2007) show that the actual reconviction rate for those released in 2004 (64.7%) was almost identical to that for those released in 2000 (64.8%). While it is laudable that the prison and probation services are being more effective with those they are sent by the courts, the bald fact is that, for most of the period that our use of custody has been increasing, reconviction rates on release have also been rising (Figure 3.4).

It is only fair to note that this may not be an entirely like-for-like comparison post 2000, but that is because the government stopped publishing simple annual reconviction rate trends in 2003. In any event, it is unlikely that changes in reconviction measurement or the inclusion of additional offences into the 'Standard List' (Home Office, 2003) explains much of the trend, as the increase in reconviction rates began at the same time that the prison population began to rise, not when measurements changed. The fact that the reconviction rates for those sentenced to community supervision does not reveal a similar pattern (see Appendix 3A) also suggests that there is a real link between the prison population and reconviction rates.

The most obvious explanation for the rise in raw reconviction rates on release from prison is that sentencers are employing custody less effectively now than they were in the early 1990s. It is quite plausible that, by sending significantly more minor offenders (for example, those convicted of theft and handling and 'other non-motoring' offences) to prison for short periods of time, they are simply disrupting offenders' lives so

Figure 3.4 The prison population and two-year prison 'raw' reconviction rates

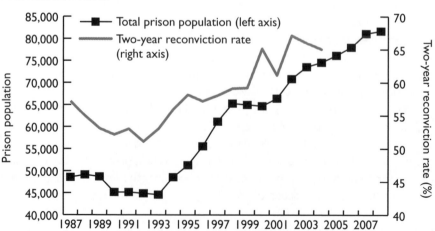

Source: Based on figures from Home Office (2003), RDS NOMS (2005, 2006, 2007a, 2007b) and Prison Service (2006, 2007, 2008)

that they lose employment and accommodation and contact with support networks (Social Exclusion Unit, 2002), without providing an opportunity in prison or in the community for any worthwhile rehabilitative work to be pursued.

The public appetite for imprisonment and the cost of feeding it

Despite improvements in the performance of crime reduction and criminal justice agencies, much of the public debate is centred on issues of punishment and fear of crime. For example:

- 65% of the public continue to believe that crime is increasing across the country as a whole;
- 79% feel that sentence lengths should not be shortened; and
- 57% feel that the number of people sent to prison should not be reduced.

(Carter, 2007, p 6)

Carter (2007) presents these figures as part of the justification for increasing the size of the prison estate without discussing why falling official crime rates as measured by the British Crime Survey (BCS) are not mirrored by improvements in public confidence; and without acknowledging that the public's views on imprisonment are not so unambiguously draconian as these statistics suggest.

While it is true that nearly two-thirds of the public still believe that crime is rising nationally, this proportion has fallen since the early 2000s (Lovebakke, 2007), perhaps suggesting that the message is finally getting through (although quite possibly at just the point where crime is likely to rise again). The most obvious reason for the continuing disjuncture is that most people know very little about actual levels of crime and assume that what is reported in the media is a comprehensive account rather than selectively focusing on the bizarre and abnormal (Pratt, 2007). Those sections of the public who rely on the popular press for their news assume that particularly horrible crimes are reported so frequently because crime is getting more serious and more prevalent, rather than that crime reporting is a useful weapon in a newspaper's battle for market share.

It is also important to recognise that perceptions of local crime are less distorted than perceptions of the national picture. Over the past 10 years, the percentage of BCS respondents who think that local crime is rising has been around 20 percentage points lower than the percentage who believe this about crime across the country. In 2006–07, for example, 41% thought that crime had increased locally compared with 65% who thought it had increased nationally (Lovebakke, 2007). This is probably because local media reporting is less feverish but also because local views are more likely to be shaped by direct personal experience and that of friends and family.

The statistics Carter selects suggest that while increasing the number of prison places 'may not offer the tax payer optimum value for money' (Carter, 2007, p 27), it is justified because it is what the public wants. But this ignores the fact that they have already been given what they want – custody has indeed been used more frequently, and for longer, even if it has not been targeted on serious offenders in the way the public expected! The money spent on building extra prisons might be spent more profitably on reassuring the public that they have been listened to – and the consequence has been increased prison reconviction rates.

There is also good reason to think that it is possible to tackle the public perception that sentencing is unduly lenient (for example, Hough and Roberts, 1999). Indeed, a careful review of the research concludes that 'The idea that there is widespread support for greater use of imprisonment and for tougher prison conditions is based on a partial and selective reading of the research evidence' (Roberts and Hough, 2005, p 301). A national campaign may be useful in spreading a more informed picture of sentencing, as Hough and Roberts (2004a, 2004b) suggest. However, given that the same review also shows that politicians are even less trusted than judges, using direct and local communication initiatives may be a more effective way of communicating just how frequently the courts now resort to custody.[9]

It is also important to recognise that the figures used by Carter to demonstrate the public's apparently insatiable demand for custody also tell only part of the story. For example, Hough and Roberts (2004b) report the results of a MORI telephone survey of 2,689 adults across England and Wales in 2003 which showed that the proportion of the public who thought that prison was effective in keeping offenders secure was twice the proportion who thought it was effective in reforming them (89% and 44%, respectively).

Also, as the Secretary of State for Justice, Jack Straw, noted in a recent speech:

> When asked what the most important issues are when it comes to crime the single most popular answer coming from 26% of those polled was that sentences are too lenient. But when asked what would most reduce crime – only 6% suggested that more offenders in prison was the answer. So when I hear journalists saying that they are simply reflecting the views of their readers I have to sometimes question their interpretation. Reporting of crime does not reflect the true picture, nor do calls for tougher sentences withstand much scrutiny. When presented with alternatives, very few people want to send more people to prison.
>
> (Speech to Guardian Criminal Justice Summit on 'Prisons, Probation and the Press', Law Society, 10 March 2007)

In an age in which the financial cost of giving life-saving drugs to cancer patients is regarded as a legitimate consideration, it is astonishing that so little of the public debate centres around whether sending more people to prison represents a cost-effective way of tacking crime and reducing reoffending. Even assuming that Carter's 2003 estimate that the 22% increase in the prison population between 1997 and 2003 led to a 5% decrease in crime is accurate – and absolutely no evidence is presented to support it – this does not mean that financing additional prison places was money well spent. A recent analysis (Matrix, 2007) has assessed the financial value of the reductions in reoffending associated with different interventions and the cost of such interventions. It concluded that the savings to the taxpayer of using a community-based intervention rather than prison ranged from just over £3,000 to about £88,000, depending on the nature of the community intervention. When the calculation included the savings resulting from fewer victim costs, the savings were between £16,000 and £202,000 per offender. Whatever its faults, the 'quality adjusted life year', or 'QALY', system used by the National Institute for Health and Clinical Excellence (NICE) at least allows the value for money of different medical treatments to be assessed on a comparable basis.[10] Creating a similar measure for assessing the extent to which criminal justice interventions secure public safety may help to move the debate about our use of imprisonment forward. Using this approach would make it possible to compare prison sentences with and without time on licence and with and without programmes. Under this approach it would be possible to take account of both the incapacitative effects of imprisonment *and* the harm it can cause (for example, loss of employment, accommodation and social ties) when assessing the value of imprisonment and when comparing it with other sentences.

It would also be advisable to learn another lesson from the field of health economics where the concept of 'supplier induced demand' is better understood. In the crudest model of supplier induced demand, physicians encourage patients to demand services which are not medically necessary because the doctors do not bear the cost but may benefit either directly in terms of income or reputation. Patients follow this advice because their knowledge of their needs is imperfect. More recent and sophisticated interpretations recognise that supplier induced demand is less commonly a function of unethical behaviour on the part of the medical profession but occurs because doctors themselves have an imperfect understanding of the medical value of the treatments available (see Richardson and Peacock, 2006). Building more prison places in a context in which not only the public but even sentencers have an imperfect understanding of the impact of custody on crime and reoffending will not lead to the demand for prison places being met; it will generate such demand.

Conclusion

Contrary to claims made in Carter (2007) report, efforts to bring more offences to justice may have contributed to the rise in the prison population, but without keeping the public any safer. The increased use of custody has been affected by the sentencing of some serious offences. The proportion of those convicted for violent and drug offences going to custody has increased overall and, on average, sentences are longer, especially for sex offences and burglary. However, the biggest change in sentencing behaviour concerns the number and length of custodial sentences for less serious property offences and cases which are too trivial (summary only) to be sent to the Crown Court. This is surely not what the public have in mind when they call for tougher sentencing.

The fact that modelled reconviction rates show that the Prison Service is doing a better job is a testament to the hard work of its staff, despite increasing overcrowding. Raw reconviction rates suggest that this is in the face of custody being used less effectively by the courts. The cost of the change in sentencing behaviour cannot be measured simply in terms of extra prison places; the extra reconvictions which have resulted also carry a cost.

In putting the case for building more prison places, Lord Carter suggests that we may have a gap between the demand for prison places and prison capacity which is 'at worst' 13,000. If, as predicted, building extra places creates demand, this is by no means the worst case scenario imaginable.

There are no new easy or quick fixes for constraining or reducing the size of the prison population. Of course, tackling sentencing drift is not the only strategy needed, but there is even less political appetite for tackling the issues around executive release. An obvious first step, given the evidence provided in this paper, would be to disentangle the idea of introducing a structured sentencing framework from the question of whether a permanent sentencing commission is needed and to introduce the framework immediately, perhaps under the aegis of the existing Sentencing Guidelines Council. Even if that is not politically viable, immediate action could be taken to limit magistrates' powers to use custody for non-violent summary offences more strictly; and specifically to discourage sentencers from using custody for theft and handling. This would not solve prison overcrowding but it would slow down the rate at which it worsens and it would ensure that fewer people were sent to prison for periods which were just long enough to further fragment their already tenuous ties with society.

Of course, any calls to limit the prison population are likely to be portrayed by the popular press negatively as being soft on crime but that is not a good enough reason to conceal the damaging financial and public safety consequences of our increasing use of custody. The way that the government has managed the news agenda on 'law and order' has been part of the problem. The consequence of pandering to 'penal populism' in the short term by building more prison places is that the financial costs of the building programme will be much greater than the forecast because it will feed rather than meet demand.

The longer-term cost of leaving penal populists to frame the debate entirely in terms of punishment versus leniency will be felt in terms of reduced public safety. Recent history suggests that if the prison population rises, reconviction rates on release will also rise. Developing a recognised measure – or 'QALY' – of public safety could help to inform and reframe the public debate so that the impact and value of different interventions can be compared in a common currency.

Finally, while it may be possible to meet the public's demand for punishment *and* for sentences which are effective in reducing reconviction, more frequently, at the level of the individual offender, this results in sentences which send out such mixed messages that neither is achieved effectively. There is good evidence to suggest that the public have a more sophisticated take on this than either government policies or media reports give them credit for. It is important to capitalise on that if imprisonment is to be used in a way which genuinely 'secures the future'.

Notes

[1] On 30 June 1998 there were 65,298 prisoners in England and Wales (Home Office, 2003). On 27 June 2008 there were 83,243 (see www.hmprisonservice.gov.uk/assets/documents/10003BD527062008_web_report.doc).

[2] The Conservative opposition under David Cameron has also signalled its support for a substantial prison-building programme in its recent policy Green Paper, *Prisons with a purpose*. See www.conservatives.com/tile.do?def=safer.greener.page

[3] Perhaps because the remand population has risen less dramatically than the sentenced population the word 'remand' does not appear at all in Carter (2003). The need to move suitable remand prisoners to bail hostels is acknowledged in Carter (2007) but only as something the 'government is already working on' (p 27).

[4] See Liebling (this volume) for a detailed critique of the 'Titan' concept.

[5] The indictable 'other non-motoring' category covers a rag-bag of offences from firearms offences to carrying offensive weapons to unlicensed wheel clamping. Summary 'other non-motoring' includes vagrancy and failure to pay a TV licence.

[6] Public Service Agreements (PSAs) were first introduced in the 1998 Comprehensive Spending Review. This set approximately 600 performance targets for around 35 areas of government. The number has been reduced and combined in successive spending reviews (Gay, 2005). The 2002 PSA target was to: 'Improve the delivery of justice by increasing the number of crimes for which an offender is brought to justice to 1.2 million by 2005–06'.

[7] Interestingly, modelled reconviction rates for the reducing re-offending PSA allow for this (see, for example, Cunliffe and Shepherd, 2007).

[8] It is to be hoped that the decision to drop analyses of sentencing by previous convictions from routine Sentencing Statistics (RDS NOMS 2007b) is a one-off and not the start of a trend. Ideally these should also include the raw reconviction rates which have not been published as a series since RDS NOMS (2005) produced

the 2004 volume of the Offender Management Statistics. It would be helpful if the Ministry of Justice reinstituted the publication of reconviction rates by length of prison sentence which was discontinued in the early 2000s.

[9] See, for example, Salisbury (2004) who found that improvements in public perception could be achieved simply by engaging people in a discussion of crime and criminal justice even before they had received more information about it.

[10] As the Select Committee on Health's recent report explains: 'A single QALY would indicate one year in perfect health. The value of a year in less than perfect health would be a fraction (for example, 0.5) of a QALY. Improvements in length and quality of life are referred to as fractions of a QALY. To assess cost-effectiveness, the QALY score is integrated with the price of treatment using the incremental cost-effectiveness ratio (ICER). This represents the change in costs in relation to the change in health status. The result is a 'cost per QALY' figure, which allows NICE to determine the cost-effectiveness of the treatment.' (House of Commons Health Committee, 2008, p 33)

References

Carter, P. (2003) *Managing offenders, reducing crime: A new approach*, London: Ministry of Justice.

Carter, P. (2007) *Securing the future: Proposals for the efficient and sustainable use of custody in England and Wales*, London: Ministry of Justice.

Cunliffe, J. and Shepherd, A. (2007) *Re-offending of adults: Results from the 2004 cohort*, Home Office Statistical Bulletin 06/07, London: Home Office.

Cuppleditch, L. and Evans, W. (2005) *Re-offending of adults: Results from the 2002 cohort*, Home Office Statistical Bulletin 25/05, London: Home Office.

Gay, O. (2005) *Public service agreements*, Parliament and Constitution Centre Standard Note: SN/PC/3826, London: House of Commons Library, www.parliament.uk/commons/lib/research/notes/snpc-03826.pdf

Hedderman, C. (2004) 'Why are more women being sentenced to custody?' in G. McIvor (ed) *Women who offend,* London: Jessica Kingsley.

Hedderman, C. (2006) 'Keeping a lid on the prison population – will NOMS help?' in M. Hough, R. Allen and U. Padel (eds) *Reshaping probation and prisons: The new offender management framework*, Bristol: The Policy Press.

Home Office (2001) *Criminal statistics, England and Wales, 2000*, London: HMSO.

Home Office (2003) *Prison statistics, England and Wales, 2002*, Command Paper 5743, London: HMSO.

Hough, M. and Roberts, J.V. (1999) 'Sentencing trends in Britain: Public knowledge and public opinion', *Punishment & Society* 1999, vol 1, issue 1, pp 11–26.

Hough, M. and Roberts, J.V. (2004a) *Confidence in justice: An international review*, London: King's College, www.kcl.ac.uk/depsta/law/research/icpr/publications/confidence%20in%20justice.pdf

Hough, M. and Roberts, J.V. (2004b) *Confidence in justice: An international review,* Findings 243, London: Home Office.

Hough, M., Jacobson, J. and Millie, A. (2003) *The decision to imprison: Sentencing and the prison population,* London: Prison Reform Trust.

House of Commons Health Committee (2008) *National Institute for Health and Clinical Excellence First Report of Session 2007–08,* HC 27-I, www.publications.parliament. uk/pa/cm200708/cmselect/cmhealth/27/27.pdf

Hudson, B. (2003) *Understanding justice: An introduction to ideas, perspectives and controversies in modern penal theory* (2nd edn), Maidenhead: Open University Press.

Kershaw, C. and Renshaw, G. (1997) *Reconvictions of prisoners discharged from prison in 1993, England and Wales,* Statistical Bulletin 5/97, London: Home Office.

Lewis, C.S. (1943) *Mere Christianity,* http://lib.ru/LEWISCL/mere_engl.txt

Lloyd, C., Mair, G. and Hough, M. (1994) *Explaining reconviction rates: A critical analysis,* Home Office Research Study 136, London: Home Office.

Lovebakke, J. (2007) 'Public Perceptions', in S. Nicholas, C. Kershaw and A. Walker (eds) *Crime in England and Wales 2006/07,* Home Office Statistical Bulletin, London: Home Office.

Matrix (2007) *The economic case for and against prison,* London: Matrix Knowledge Group.

Pratt, J. (2007) *Penal populism,* London: Routledge.

Prison Service (2006) *Prison population bulletin June 2006,* www.hmprisonservice.gov. uk/assets/documents/10001DF1pop_bull_june_06.doc

Prison Service (2007) *Prison population bulletin June 2007,* www.hmprisonservice.gov. uk/assets/documents/10002C60pop_bull_jun_07.doc

Prison Service (2008) *Prison population bulletin, March 2008,* www.hmprisonservice. gov.uk/assets/documents/100037DDmonthly_bulletin_mar08.doc

RDS NOMS (2004) *Offender management statistics, 2003,* Home Office Statistical Bulletin 15/04, London: Home Office.

RDS NOMS (2005) *Offender management statistics, 2004,* Home Office Statistical Bulletin 17/05, London: Home Office.

RDS NOMS (2006) *Offender management statistics, 2005,* Home Office Statistical Bulletin 18/06, London: Home Office.

RDS NOMS (2007a) *Sentencing statistics, 2005,* Home Office Statistical Bulletin 03/07, London: Home Office.

RDS NOMS (2007b) *Sentencing statistics, 2006,* London: Ministry of Justice.

Richardson, J. and Peacock, S. (2006) *Reconsidering theories and evidence of supplier-induced demand,* Centre for Health Economics Research Paper 2006 (13), Clayton: Monash University, www.buseco.monash.edu.au/centres/che/pubs/rp13.pdf

Roberts, J.V. and Hough, M. (2005) 'The state of prisons: exploring public knowledge and opinion', *The Howard Journal,* vol 44, no 3, pp 286–306.

Salisbury, H. (2004) *Public attitudes to the criminal justice system: The impact of providing information to British crime survey respondents,* on-line report 64/04, www. homeoffice.gov.uk/rds/pdfs04/rdsolr6404.pdf

Shepherd, A. and Whiting, E. (2006) 'Re-offending of adults: results from the 2003 cohort', Home Office Statistical Bulletin 20/06, London: Home Office.

Social Exclusion Unit (2002) *Reducing re-offending by ex-prisoners*, London: Office of the Deputy Prime Minister.

Spicer, K. and Glicksman, A. (2004) *Adult reconviction: Results from the 2001 cohort*, online report 59/04, London: Home Office.

Straw, J. (2008) *Prisons, probation and the press*, speech to Guardian Criminal Justice Summit, Law Society, 10 March, www.justice.gov.uk/news/sp100308a.htm

Walker, N. (1991) *Why punish?* Oxford: Oxford University Press.

Appendix 3A

Probation caseload and two-year reconviction rates for community sentences

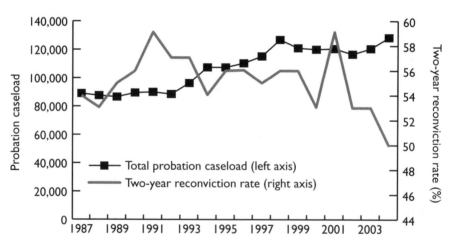

Note: For the reasons given earlier in this chapter, it is not meaningful to compare raw prison and probation reconviction rates to draw conclusions about the effectiveness of either service.

Towards more consistent and predictable sentencing in England and Wales

4

Jessica Jacobson, Julian Roberts and Mike Hough

The structure of sentencing guidelines in England and Wales is likely to undergo a significant transformation following publication of the final report of the Sentencing Commission Working Group. The Working Group has rejected the creation of a US-style sentencing commission for England and Wales (2008b),[1] having made clear in its consultation paper that it had also decided against the introduction of a US-style sentencing grid for this jurisdiction (Sentencing Commission Working Group, 2008a). Both decisions are consistent with the submissions made to the Working Group (see Sentencing Commission Working Group (2008c) for a summary). Time will tell, but it seems likely that the government will now proceed to implement the Working Group's recommendations to fuse the Sentencing Advisory Panel (SAP) and the Sentencing Guidelines Council (SGC) and to enhance the resources, profile and functions of the new agency. Where do these developments leave us?

In this chapter we offer some commentary on issues surrounding sentencing guidelines in England and Wales, and suggest some ways in which sentencing in this jurisdiction may be enhanced still further. We focus on a small number of important questions: (i) what kinds of sentencing guidelines are appropriate for England and Wales? (ii) is the current 'departure' test for sentences falling outside the guidelines adequate to ensure a sufficient level of compliance with the guidelines? (iii) should sentencing guidelines be sensitive to prison capacity, and if so how? and (iv) should a guidelines authority such as the SGC have a community engagement function, as is the case with sentencing authorities in some other jurisdictions? Our answers to these critical questions are preceded by a brief discussion of the nature of the problem to which sentencing guidelines are a response, and a review of the nature of sentencing guidelines in this country and elsewhere.

The problem of prison overuse

The problem of prison overuse has been well-documented (see Hedderman, this volume). Since the early 1990s, the number of offenders sentenced by the courts has been broadly static. Crime rates for many offences have fallen steeply, yet the prison population has almost doubled since 1992, rising more rapidly than at any time since 1945. We have obviously made a value judgement in characterising these trends as representing an *overuse* of custodial sentences. It is not our purpose here to argue the case for this position, but we simply direct interested readers to von Hirsch et al

(1999) and Bottoms et al (2004) for reviews and to Spelman (2005) for a US-based cost benefit analysis of the use of imprisonment.

The immediate causes of the growth in the prison population can be stated simply: since 1992 the sentencing process has become tougher in all respects (see Hedderman, this volume, for details). There are several reasons for this. First, sentencers and other penal decision-makers have responded to statutory changes introducing new penalties or tougher variants of existing ones. Second, the climate of media and public opinion about law and order has almost certainly made penal decision-makers more risk-averse (see Hough et al, 2003). One can argue about whether the media have created or simply exploited these misperceptions. Whatever the case, the end-result is a climate of debate about law and order that traps politicians in what Nicola Lacey describes in this volume as 'prisoners' dilemma'.[2] A state of mutual distrust prevents constructive agreement on the best ways of punishing offenders. The key to solving the problem of prison overcrowding is, first and foremost, to find a political solution to this intrinsically political problem: politicians need help in finding a constructive resolution to their particular 'prisoners' dilemma'. In this respect a sentencing council can play an important part.

What kind of guidance is needed in England and Wales?

The current guidelines system

The 1998 Crime and Disorder Act gave the Court of Appeal Criminal Division (CACD) formal powers to formulate and issue guideline judgements.[3] It also established the Sentencing Advisory Panel, which had the statutory function of providing advice to the CACD, either proactively or reactively. This Act thus constituted an important step towards the establishment of structures and procedures designed to improve sentencing consistency and (potentially, at least) to inject a degree of cost-consciousness into judicial decision making. The 2003 Criminal Justice Act created the Sentencing Guidelines Council. The Sentencing Advisory Panel was left in place, but was required to provide advice to the SGC rather than to the CACD. Provisions of the 2003 Act impose a duty on sentencers to 'have regard to' SGC guidance (s. 172) and to state reasons for deviating from SGC guidance when it does so (s. 174(2)a) (these provisions will be discussed later in this chapter). As matters now stand in England and Wales, the principal source of sentencing guidance is therefore the SGC, although the CACD and the Judicial Studies Board are also both significant – the latter through its training function.

Guidance for sentencers in this jurisdiction is organised broadly around the concept of proportionality, where punishment is proportional to the harm committed and the offender's level of culpability. The guidance usually takes the form of dividing the offence into bands of different gravity, and setting out starting points and

Box 4.1: Illustration of SGC guidelines

Street robbery or 'mugging'
Robberies of small businesses
Less sophisticated commercial robberies

Robbery is a serious offence for the purposes of sections 225 and 227 Criminal Justice Act 2003

Maximum Penalty: **Life imprisonment**

ADULT OFFENDERS

Type/nature of activity	Starting point	Sentencing range
The offence includes the threat or use of minimal force and removal of property	12 months custody	Up to 3 years custody
A weapon is produced and used to threaten, and/or force is used which results in injury to the victim	4 years custody	2-7 years custody
The victim is caused serious physical injury by the use of significant force and/or use of a weapon	8 years custody	7-12 years custody

Additional aggravating factors	Additional mitigating factors
1. More than one offender involved. 2. Being the ringleader of a group of offenders. 3. Restraint, detention or additional degradation, of the victim. 4. Offence was pre-planned. 5. Wearing a disguise. 6. Offence committed at night. 7. Vulnerable victim targeted. 8. Targeting of large sums of money or valuable goods. 9. Possession of a weapon that was not used.	1. Unplanned/opportunistic. 2. Peripheral involvement. 3. Voluntary return of property taken. 4. Clear evidence of remorse. 5. Ready co-operation with the police.

Source: www.sentencing-guidelines.gov.uk/docs/robbery-guidelines.pdf

sentence length ranges for each band. Guidance is also provided with respect to some aggravating and mitigating factors that should be taken into account. As noted, deviation from the proposed range is permitted, provided that reasons are stated. The guidance is based upon the case of a first-time offender pleading not guilty.[4] As an example, Box 4.1 sets out the SGC's guidance for the offence of robbery.

The guidelines produced by the SGC represent a considerable achievement, given that the body has been in existence for less than four years. However, the system of developing definitive guidelines has some weaknesses. First, the process of consulting Parliament and the wider public is lengthy. Second, the piecemeal approach of dealing with offence groups sequentially rather than concurrently may result in inconsistencies between guidelines for different offences both in substantive terms and in terms of process and format (see discussion in Hirst, 2008).

A third – and critical – problem is that there is currently no way of knowing whether a new guideline, properly implemented, represents a shift up or down tariff in relation to existing practice. Even if there was political will to use the current guideline system as a means for controlling judicial demand for prison places, there is not enough information available to know precisely what impact any given set of detailed guidance would achieve if fully implemented. Perhaps the most important problem is that levels of compliance with the guidelines are not monitored. We do not know to what extent the guidelines are followed – a subject we shall return to later in this chapter. Finally, the two bodies (the SGC and the SAP) lack much public visibility. If their function is defined in fairly narrow terms – as the provision of sentencing guidance – this is not a significant problem. However, the more that they are required to engage in public debate, the more important it is that they should be able to command authority and public trust.[5]

Sentencing guidelines and guideline authorities in other jurisdictions

In the US, sentencing guidelines typically take the form of a grid composed of two dimensions, representing what are taken – in those jurisdictions – to be the two most important determinants of sentence severity: crime seriousness and the offender's criminal history. Sentencing grids exist in various forms across the US, and have been proposed in at least one other jurisdiction (Western Australia). Although popular in the US, they were rejected as a model in New Zealand (2002), Canada (1987), and South Africa (2000) for varying reasons.[6] Some of the US systems are presumptive in nature – sentencers are required to follow the guideline range or explain why they have deviated. Other systems are voluntary in nature, existing simply to provide guidance to courts rather than to exercise control over sentencing outcomes.[7]

Sentencing commissions and councils in other countries have a variety of functions. Commissions in Australia are involved in the production of guidance for sentencers, but their role in this respect is typically advisory – to the Court of Appeal – rather than prescriptive. Like the US systems, they have an explicit role in the provision of research and statistics both to assess the demand for prison places and to improve understanding of the sentencing process. In contrast to the US systems, they also place emphasis on consultation with the wider public, in order to incorporate community views into the sentencing process, and on informing the public about sentencing.[8] New Zealand is the latest country to create a sentencing guidelines authority, and since it reflects the experience in many other jurisdictions, it provides a useful model on which to draw (see Law Commission of New Zealand, 2006; Young, 2008; Young and Browning, 2008). The remit of its Sentencing Council stretches from the provision of guidance to community engagement, with a view to improving public confidence in sentencing.

In most western European jurisdictions, sentencing practice is guided by their respective penal codes rather than by sentencing councils or commissions, and the extent of discretion permitted to sentencers varies from country to country (for a discussion of European jurisdictions the reader is directed to the review by the Sentencing Commission for Scotland (2006)).

Should England and Wales adopt a presumptively binding sentencing grid?

Guidelines systems that are highly presumptive and structured, like those of many states in the US, offer some clear benefits. For one thing, they make the sentencing process more transparent. This level of clarity also results in greater overall predictability of sentencing outcomes in the aggregate. Projections of sentencing patterns are likely to be more accurate and this permits the guidelines authority to be able to predict and – in jurisdictions where they have the mandate – to control the prison population. Finally, by providing a structured guidelines environment that encompasses all (or most) offences, the guidelines authority is able to ensure that legislative or guidelines amendments result in a holistic transformation of sentencing practices.[9]

However, presumptive sentencing grids also have a number of serious disadvantages. First, depending on the degree of structure, crimes of quite variable seriousness may end up being assigned a common seriousness level. This means that a degree of proportionality is inevitably lost. In the pursuit of reducing *unwarranted disparity*, these systems can generate the opposite problem, namely *unwarranted uniformity*. This arises when unlike cases are treated alike. In particular, the US grids allow little scope for sentencers to take account of culpability factors that relate to the offender's circumstances, in a way that is now required in this jurisdiction by the 2003 Criminal Justice Act.

Second (and linked to the first problem), sentencing grids tend to project a rather mechanical or formulaic image of the sentencing decision. Many people, not just judges, see the determination of sentence as a 'human process', one in which the specific characteristics of the individual offender must be considered. Third, it is sometimes suggested that detailed sentencing manuals may discourage courts from considering cases in sufficient detail; they may simply impose a sentence within the guideline range. Fourth, by making the outcomes of conviction specific, numerical grids encourage and facilitate plea bargaining. By specifying the offence to which the offender is prepared to plead guilty, defence counsel can, in effect, identify the sentence that the offender is prepared to accept without contesting guilt. Fifth, and linked to this, sentencing grids may encourage dishonesty in sentencing, in that judges can 'work back' from the sentence that they think is fair to an assessment of the appropriate 'facts of the case'. Sixth, presumptive or grid-style guidelines are typically unpopular with judges trained in the common law tradition that permits considerable judicial discretion at sentencing.[10]

Finally, a grid along the US lines formalises – and may promote to an excessive degree – the role of previous convictions. All jurisdictions place heavy emphasis on the seriousness of the crime as the principal sentencing factor, but there is less consensus about the role of previous convictions (Roberts, 2008). We agree therefore with the Working Group (and, it would appear, most judges and other parties who made submissions to the Group) that any form of sentencing guidelines grid is unlikely to prove acceptable either to criminal justice professionals (including and especially sentencers) or to the public in this country. Despite their ability to achieve specific policy goals rapidly, sentencing grids have more disadvantages than advantages for a jurisdiction such as England and Wales.

What alternatives are there?

If formal two-dimensional presumptive sentencing grids are not the answer, what other options exist? Although many people associate grid structures with the US, in fact guideline schemes across that jurisdiction can take many other forms. One of the leading guidelines experts in the US has written that the approaches to structuring sentencing 'are almost as numerous as the jurisdictions adopting them' (Frase, 2005a, p 1191; see also Frase, 2000).[11] A critical variable in the US is the level of constraint imposed upon sentencers. Some guidelines are presumptive in nature – with some scope for departure – while others are merely advisory. The latter inevitably have less impact on sentencing practice than presumptive schemes (for example, Tonry, 1996; Ostrom et al, 2008). At the same time, they do achieve some purchase on sentencers' decision making, without the problems of overprescription (see Hunt and Connelly, 2005). At present, research has yet to reach a definitive answer regarding the relative merits of the two systems.[12]

One area in which presumptively binding guideline schemes appear to have an advantage concerns resource management, or management of the prison estate. Reitz (2005), among several other authorities, notes that presumptive regimes have had more success in managing prison populations than voluntary guideline schemes. But the latter are not totally ineffective in addressing this issue, as the experience in Missouri has demonstrated. In that state, judges enjoy wide discretion at sentencing, without appellate review, as long as the sentence is within the statutory limit. However, judges are provided with sentencing recommendations as well as a range of other information to guide their decision making. Preliminary data on the impact of this advisory package[13] has suggested a decrease in the prison population (Wolff, 2006).

The Canadian experience also has some lessons to offer. In 1987, the Canadian Sentencing Commission published its final report, recommending the creation of a permanent sentencing commission. It proposed a novel guidelines scheme, one that may be considered a hybrid approach to structuring discretion (Canadian Sentencing Commission, 1987). In the event, neither the recommended commission nor the guideline scheme was actually adopted.[14] Nevertheless, the scheme is worth noting as an alternative to the numerical grids used across the US.[15]

What would best suit England and Wales?

We agree with the Working Group that the revamped SGC should retain the SGC model of definitive guidelines. Consider the SGC's guidelines for robbery, summarised above. The offence is stratified into three sub-categories, with examples of the kinds of conduct which are typical of each. The guideline provides starting points and sentence ranges applicable to each level, and provides a non-exhaustive list of mitigating and aggravating factors. The guidance also includes a commentary. The degree of guidance is substantial, yet courts retain a significant degree of discretion to sentence outside the guideline range.[16] Moreover, a number of advantages arise as a result of using the existing SGC guidelines as the basis of the guidance promulgated by a revamped council. First, the degree of specificity of the existing guidelines is appropriate, given that it is loose enough to permit considerable judicial discretion in the passing of sentence[17] (and the avoidance of unwarranted uniformity), but detailed enough to structure and inform sentencing decisions in a meaningful way. Second, the existing guidelines have been developed through an exhaustive process of consultation, and in the absence of any evidence to the contrary we would assume that their content is broadly acceptable to the judiciary and the wider public. Third, and from a more pragmatic standpoint, it would be difficult to justify the resources that would have to be invested in any thoroughgoing revision of the guidelines, especially given that they were all recently devised.

Finally, it is important to acknowledge the importance of judicial reaction to any proposal to amend the nature of sentencing guidelines in this jurisdiction. If the judiciary are opposed to the guidelines, or some element of the guidance offered, compliance rates will be low. It is clear from the submissions to the Working Group's consultation paper that the judiciary in England and Wales are strongly opposed to the introduction of a sentencing grid, and that there is significant support for the current guidelines format provided by the Sentencing Guidelines Council (see Sentencing Commission Working Group, 2008c).

How binding should guidelines be upon courts?

Independent of the nature of the guidelines, it is important to establish the degree of constraint imposed upon courts. In our view, although there may be little reason to alter the basic content and degree of structure of the existing SGC guidelines, there is a case for making the guidelines more presumptive. The degree of constraint should depend upon the breadth of the guidelines; if the guideline range is very broad, there is a greater necessity for sentencers to conform. On the other hand, a higher departure rate would be expected, and indeed desirable, if the guidelines prescribe a very narrow range of sentence lengths.

At present the 'departure' provisions in the 2003 Criminal Justice Act state that 'In sentencing an offender, every court must have regard to any guidelines which are relevant to the offender's case' (s. 172), and 'Where guidelines indicate that a sentence of a particular kind, or within a particular range, would normally be appropriate for the offence and the sentence is of a different kind, or is outside that range, state the court's reasons for deciding on a sentence of a different kind or outside that range' (s. 174(2)).

Are these provisions sufficiently directive to ensure that courts consistently follow the guidelines? The statutory requirement for the courts to impose a sentence while 'having regard to' the Council's guidelines is in no way comparable to the 'presumptiveness' of many guideline schemes operating across the US. The Sentencing Commission Working Group recommended a change to the test for departures, namely replacing the current 'have regard to' wording with a provision which would allow a court to pass a sentence outside the guidelines only if it is of the opinion that it 'is in the interests of justice' to do so (Sentencing Commission Working Group, 2008b, p 32). This language is derived from the New Zealand sentencing guideline proposals. In our view, the modified wording proposed by the Working Group is unlikely to result in a lower 'departure rate' – whatever that rate is, since at present we have no idea what proportion of sentences fall within the SGC guidelines.

It may well be the case that no modification of the language articulating the departure test will greatly affect the departure rate; words alone cannot achieve or even enhance compliance. However, we feel that to the extent that different formulations do translate into different levels of compliance, the stronger language of the Minnesota guidelines is more appropriate. Under the guidelines in that state, a court may depart from the guidelines only if the sentencing judge finds and records 'substantial and compelling circumstances that make the departure more appropriate than the presumptive sentence' (Minnesota Sentencing Guidelines Commission, 2007, p 30). We are of the view that tightening the language of these provisions in this way would not have the effect of overly curtailing judicial discretion, or producing unwarranted uniformity, since the guidelines' ranges themselves are wider than their US counterparts. However, although we prefer this stronger form of test, it is possible that this departure test would provoke judicial opposition.

Should sentencing guidelines be sensitive to prison capacity?

Should sentencing guidelines be sensitive to prison capacity, and if so, in what specific ways? US sentencing guidelines are usually sensitive to prison capacity, with adjustments made to sentence ranges in response to prison overcrowding. States that have adopted this approach to their sentencing guidelines – which represent a minority of jurisdictions across the US – have largely been successful in avoiding prison overcrowding, and without recourse to 'one-off' remedial strategies such as amnesties or introducing ad hoc changes to the early release system. Minnesota is generally recognised to be among the most successful, while the federal system has been widely criticised, not least by the Supreme Court, which ruled that its mandatory requirements were unconstitutional. Despite the original intention of insulating sentencing from politics, the Commission was captive to political pressures, and issued highly punitive guidance (Gertner, 2008).

As noted earlier, at the time of writing (July 2008) the Law Commission of New Zealand was developing sentencing and parole guidelines for that jurisdiction. With respect to correctional capacity and guidelines, the New Zealand proposal involves what may be termed an indirect relationship between the two. Proposed legislation (the Sentencing Council Act) will require the sentencing guidelines council to assess and publish the impact of its guidelines upon prison populations. Parliament is then able to consider the guidelines in light of the costs that they will likely generate. In the event that Parliament passes a resolution to 'disapply' the guidelines, the effect of this would be to require the sentencing council to reconsider them (see Young and Browning, 2008).

Position of the Sentencing Commission Working Group

In its consultation paper the Sentencing Commission Working Group was guarded about the relationship between sentencing guidance and prison capacity, suggesting simply that a system of guidelines should not be seen as a 'short term adjustment tool to dampen current demand' (Sentencing Commission Working Group, 2008a, p 3). In its final report the Working Group came to the view that 'currently in the absence of sufficient baseline data on sentencing practice it is not practicable to impose a duty on the SGC to draw up a framework designed to fit within current and reasonably foreseeable capacity' (2008b, p 28). And further: 'The majority of the Working Group believes that the disadvantages of placing a duty on the SGC to have regard to resources outweigh the advantages' (2008b, p 29).

Difficulties of linking guidelines and prison capacity

The prospect of a sentencing guidelines authority fulfilling the penal equivalent of the Bank of England's Monetary Policy Committee[18] raises issues of both principle and practicality. The issues of principle relate to the containment of sentencing disparity, which has served as one of the central rationales for sentencing commissions. Given this overarching purpose, it may seem odd to design a system with an inbuilt capacity to vary sentencing severity over time – and thus create *temporal* disparity – at the same time that it restricts geographic disparity (that is, unprincipled variation between courts across the country). Pragmatic decisions to adjust the sentencing tariff to fit the Treasury pocket may appear unprincipled – and may carry a significant political price tag.

On the other hand it strikes us as equally unrealistic to take the position that resource considerations must *never* enter into decisions about penal policy – especially given the unplanned and uncontrolled upward drift in sentencing over much of the last 15 years.[19] Whatever the political costs in doing so, we think it justifiable for Parliament to review periodically, in the light of affordability and other issues, whether the sentencing process is costing an excessive amount of public funds. Inevitably, such a task would be complicated by the increasing use of indeterminate sentences, such as the sentence of imprisonment for public protection (IPP).

However, there are practical problems in actually achieving the sort of recalibration of the tariff that such a review might imply. As noted, there is currently no information about the degree of judicial compliance with SGC guidelines. Because of the lack of information on sentencing practice in general, we cannot even say for certain whether specific guidelines would be inflationary or deflationary in their impact if they achieved 100% compliance. Obviously the SGC and SAP are best placed to make assessments about current practice and to reach judgements about preferred practice. But these judgements are not formed against a backdrop of firm statistical evidence about the operation of the system.

One route to achieving the predictability that is required for this sort of recalibration is to monitor judicial practice and its concordance with SGC guidelines. This would involve an incremental – and thus slow – process of monitoring and iterative adjustment to bring guidance and sentencing practice into close alignment; periodic recalibration of the tariff could then follow. Precisely how the relevant body of statistical evidence might be accumulated and used more widely is discussed elsewhere (see Hough and Jacobson, 2008). Whatever the detail of so doing, this strikes us as representing the best way forward. The alternative – which may seem more attractive to the Ministry of Justice – is to introduce an entirely new form of guidance with enough structure and binding force to achieve predictability in one fell swoop. In our view this is a risky strategy which would privilege the Ministry of Justice's desire for predictability over and above considerations of justice that require sentencers to have sufficient discretion to take into account all relevant factors when passing sentence (cf Ashworth, 2008).

To summarise, we would propose that the revamped SGC devise its guidelines in the way that it has been doing, independent of capacity issues. At some future point,[20] however, Parliament may wish to assess whether the prison population is being inflated by the guidelines. The outcome of this review might be a comprehensive revision of the guidelines to lower prison expenditure.

Monitoring usage of the guidelines

Most sentencing commissions are tasked with collecting, analysing or publishing statistical information. As discussed above, a significant weakness in the current system in England and Wales is that there is no information about the levels of judicial compliance with SGC guidance and no way of knowing what impact any given guideline has on prison capacity. The SGC guidelines indicate what sentence an offender *ought* to expect, but provide no insight as to whether that sentence is actually passed. What is needed – by the SGC, by politicians and their officials, and by others with an interest in penal issues – is some indication of the degree of judicial compliance with the guidelines. In our view, it is unacceptable to have a system of judicial guidance that has no mechanism whatsoever for monitoring its impact.

There is only one sure way of securing this information within the current sentencing framework. Sentencers need to record, for the principal offence under sentence, how their sentence maps onto the guidance. Minimally, there needs to be a record made of:

- The judge's assessment of the severity band of the offence;
- What premium, if any, was added for prior criminal history;
- What discount, if any, the offender received for entering a guilty plea;
- Whether, taking these three factors into account, the sentence fell within the relevant SGC sentencing range;
- If the sentence did *not* fall within the sentencing range, the reasons for this 'departure' from the guideline;
- The most important mitigating and aggravating factors found by the court.

This record could be made only by the sentencing judge, or by someone making a note of his or her sentencing comments. It cannot be constructed or extrapolated from administrative records.[21] This is because it includes subjective judgements which only the sentencer can disclose. It would not take long to complete and would allow statistics to be generated of the extent of judicial compliance with guidelines. It would identify guidelines which secure high levels of compliance and those that do not. Where compliance was low, this might indicate either a need to adjust the guidance or to adjust sentencing practice. The ultimate aim should be to bring guidance and practice into alignment by a process of mutual accommodation.

We recognise that designing and putting in place the necessary recording processes is far from straightforward. There are particular problems: first, in identifying the principal offence when offenders are sentenced for several offences and, second, in describing how the sentence is apportioned between the principal conviction, any secondary convictions and any offences 'taken into consideration' (often referred to as 'TICs'). The 'totality principle' – that the aggregate sentence for a group of similar offences should remain within the overall range for the offence type in question – properly ensures that sentences for secondary offences cannot simply be calculated in isolation and then summed. However, this creates difficulties for anyone wishing to establish or monitor the degree of correspondence between guidelines and practice.

Assessing the impact of new penal policies

Most US sentencing commissions have some responsibility for assessing the impact of changes in sentencing policy and of the introduction of new sentences. This is an important function for penal policy and one that should be assumed by a sentencing authority such as the SGC. Historically, central government in England and Wales has been very poor at assessing the costs of changes to the penal process. For example, the Home Office projections for prison places required by sentences of imprisonment for public protection (IPPs) were woeful underestimates, and no proper financial provision was made for programmes for IPP prisoners. Projections of the take-up of suspended sentence orders also fell far short of reality. The reason is simple: government spending departments have an interest in getting their ministers' proposals through the Treasury, and they often underestimate the costs of these proposals. 'Overcosted' government projects are almost unheard of. For sentencing policy the solution is to place this function of 'impact assessment' with the Sentencing Guidelines Council. The task involves a mix of informed judgement and statistical modelling. For example, assessing the impact of IPPs requires modelling, to assess the size of the pool of eligible offenders, and judgement, to assess judicial 'take-up' rates.

Projecting the overall demand for prison places

Much of the discussion about sentencing guidelines has focused on the need to contain the rising prison population. The Working Group placed particular importance on the need to make accurate middle-term projections of the need for prison places, enabling government to keep supply and demand in balance (Sentencing Commission Working Group, 2008a). Aligning supply and demand for correctional resources other than prison places has also been seen as an important goal. We believe that a sentencing guidelines authority should, through its research and monitoring exercises, contribute to the task of undertaking prison population projections. However, we doubt that such a body should take on central responsibility for this, as it requires competence that runs far beyond sentencing expertise.

Projections of the prison population require assumptions to be made about:

- Crime trends
- Clear-up rates
- Prosecution and conviction rates
- Remand trends
- Sentencing trends
- Parole and licence recall rates (and length of time prisoners are held on recall)
- Breach rates
- Arrangements for home detention curfew and early release
- Transfers of foreign national prisoners.

The existing prison projections prepared by Ministry of Justice statisticians incorporate assumptions about most of these trends, and draw on several models in so doing.[22] Pre-court factors including crime trends and conviction rates probably contribute only marginally to the projections, and the major predictor variables appear at present to be related to sentencing. This reflects the fact that court workloads have been very largely static over the last 15 years – despite steep increases in crime in the early 1990s, and steep falls since the mid-1990s. Our prediction is that pre-trial factors will probably become much more salient in these projections over the next 10 or 20 years – largely because we appear to be entering a phase of global economic and social instability which is likely to trigger rises in crime rates. Whatever the case, it does not make sense to place responsibility for such projections with a *sentencing* council when many factors other than sentencing practice drive the demand for prison places.

To what extent should community engagement be a function of the SGC?

One area in which we depart from the recommendations of the Sentencing Commission Working Group concerns the issue of community education and engagement. We have discussed how politicians have locked themselves into a counterproductive competition of offering ever-tougher criminal policies to the electorate. Part of the dynamic behind this process is that a large majority of the population has very negative views about sentencers and sentencing. Most people think that sentencers are too soft, that judges and magistrates are out of touch, that the courts are unlikely to use prison for serious crimes such as burglary, robbery, rape and causing death by dangerous driving (see Roberts and Hough, 2005, pp 68–85). These beliefs are all contestable, and the public's estimates about the use of custody are simply wrong. Moreover, a large body of research on attitudes to sentencing has established that the public frequently favour more lenient sentencing options when they are provided with information about specific cases, the costs of custody, and alternatives to custody.[23] Hence media representations of a public demanding ever harsher punishment are overly simplistic.

The obvious thing to do is to try to correct public misperceptions about sentencing. However, for two reasons politicians are reluctant to do so. First, it is politically risky to tell the electorate that they have 'got it wrong', and it is especially risky to do so when the opposition will seize upon this as an example of complacency and lack of political will to tackle crime. Second, politicians probably judge — accurately — that they and their civil servants command insufficient credibility with the public to be able to persuade them about the realities of current sentencing practice. After all, they would be competing with the mass media, many sections of which are committed to attacks on the judiciary.

The spiral of penal populism has to date proved an intractable problem. However, we think that if the revamped Sentencing Guidelines Council were to be provided with sufficient powers and resources it could form part of the solution. The question to ask is whether it would be possible for government to construct an independent sentencing institution that could engage with the public more constructively than politicians and government — or indeed than the senior judiciary. A body that could evolve into the principal source of trusted information about sentencing could be of great value in helping to create a more constructive climate of public debate on penal issues.

This proposal carries obvious risks. The US Sentencing Commission was originally set up with the intention that it should insulate sentencing from politics, but in the event the body was subject to political influence, and served to make penal politics in that jurisdiction even more 'prison-centric'. It is also possible that an outward-facing sentencing council could be dismissed as an 'arm's length' spin-doctoring institution. To have credibility and authority, a commission would have to recognise and address problems when these are real. However, the recent history of penal politics in Britain is in large part a sorry tale of ignorance, misinformation and prejudice, and the need for some sort of effective counterbalancing body strikes us as clear.

Clearly there would need to be a proper demarcation between issues that fall to the SGC and those that properly fall to the legislature. Judgements about the overall framework of punishment within the criminal law are essentially political ones that should fall neither to the judiciary nor to those involved in the administration of justice. Such judgements include decisions about the appropriate severity of the *system*, as distinct from those concerned with the appropriate punishment for *specific cases*. Such political decisions need to be made democratically by the government of the day, which should in turn be accountable to Parliament. A sentencing guidelines authority should never aim to be a substitute for these political processes. But there remains an important role for a trusted institution that can explain to the public, to the media and to other interested parties how and why the sentencing process actually operates.

Conclusion

The Sentencing Commission Working Group has recommended that the existing SAP and SGC be combined in a single body with an enhanced profile, functions and resources. The earlier suggestion that a US-style 'grid' system of sentencing guidelines should be established met with widespread and vociferous opposition from consultees, and has been discarded by the Working Group. Consequently, the Working Group envisages a sentencing framework based on an extension of narrative guidelines of the kind currently devised and promulgated by the SGC. We are in agreement with the Working Group – and its consultees – about the inappropriateness of a presumptive sentencing grid for this jurisdiction. The advantages associated with a grid system, notably greater predictability in sentencing practice, appear to be strongly outweighed by the potential problems, which include unwarranted uniformity of sentencing.

However, a case can be made for introducing more restrictive grounds for departure from the guidance than are currently conveyed in the 2003 Criminal Justice Act direction to courts to 'have regard to' the SGC guidelines when passing sentence. The Working Group recommends replacing the 'have regard to' wording with a provision that would permit courts to depart from a guideline only when it is 'in the interests of justice' to do so. We are doubtful that this change of wording would have much effect on levels of compliance with the guidelines, and recommend consideration of a more robust departure test.

Currently there is no monitoring of levels of judicial compliance with the SGC guidelines. We view this as a significant weakness of the current system, and strongly recommend that a mechanism be developed for monitoring the impact of sentencing guidelines. This would permit the enhanced SGC to engage in an incremental process of iterative adjustment to bring guidance and sentencing practice into close alignment. It would also enable Parliament to assess, in due course, whether the prison population is being inflated by the guidelines and, if necessary, initiate a comprehensive revision of the guidelines to lower prison expenditure.

Although this was not an issue addressed by the Working Group, we are of the opinion that a key function of an enhanced SGC should be to engage with the public. By providing the public with reliable, detailed and user-friendly information on sentencing, as well as undertaking public consultation on guidelines, the SGC could generate constructive debate about sentencing and thereby help to break the spiral of penal populism.

Notes
[1] For a discussion of the merits of creating a sentencing commission, the reader is directed to Hough and Jacobson (2008).

[2] See also Lacey (2008). There are several variants of the prisoners' dilemma in game theory. Typically, two participants are required to play the roles of suspects under

interrogation for armed bank robbery. They face the choice of betraying the other or staying silent. If both stay silent, they face a six-month sentence for possession of firearms. If each betrays the other, they both face five years in prison. If only one betrays the other, he goes free and his co-conspirator gets 10 years. The dilemma illustrates problems of trust in competitive situations: mutual distrust results in mutual betrayal, and thus in sub-optimal outcomes for both participants.

[3] Although this was a practice that the CACD had already initiated.

[4] In practice most offenders appearing at the Crown Court for this offence will have significant criminal histories, and this will increase the severity of their sentence from the starting point. On the other hand, those who plead guilty at the earliest possible stage will also get a discount of up to a third, drawing the sentence back down again.

[5] There is a counter-argument worth noting. If the guidelines were developed in a more publicly visible manner, the process may become more political. At present the SAP and the SGC are able to develop their guidelines, and conduct consultations on their proposals, without attracting a great deal of media or political attention, and some might argue that this is a better way to proceed.

[6] The most common reason would appear to be that the guidelines are too restrictive and the architecture of the grid too rigid. New Zealand also decided that culpability was a more important structuring dimension than criminal history.

[7] See Ostrom et al (2008) for a comparative assessment of three states.

[8] The Sentencing Advisory Panel considers community views by commissioning public opinion studies, the results of which are then considered by the Panel as it devises its recommendations to the SGC. Examples of this research can be found on the SGC website (www.sentencing-guidelines.gov.uk); see also Roberts et al (2008).

[9] For example, after the introduction of the sentencing guidelines in the state of Minnesota, two important policy goals were rapidly achieved: first, racial differences between black and white defendants were reduced, and second, the nature of the custodial population was transformed. Prior to the creation of the guidelines, property offenders accounted for a high proportion of custodial admissions. After the guidelines were introduced, violent offenders accounted for a higher proportion of admissions, reflecting the state legislature's desire to punish violent offenders more harshly. Indeed, race, gender and class biases were largely eliminated as sources of disparity of outcome following the introduction of guidelines (see discussion in Frase, 2005b).

[10] Judicial opposition to sentencing guideline grids was a major factor in the rejection of such arrangements in the Canadian context; see Canadian Sentencing Commission (1987).

[11] A good overview of state sentencing guidelines schemes can be found in Kauder et al. (1997). See also the National Association of State Sentencing Commissions (list of associations available at www.ussc.gov/states/nascaddr.htm).

[12] Indeed, Hunt and Connelly argue that 'the paucity of reliable scientific evidence regarding the performance of all sentencing systems [constitutes] a major obstacle to informed choice' (2008, p 13).

[13] It is described by the Chair of the Missouri Sentencing Advisory Commission as a 'discretionary, information-based system' (see Wolff, 2006).

[14] In 1996, the Canadian parliament approved a sentencing reform bill which, *inter alia*, codified the purposes and principles of sentencing and introduced a number of other statutory reforms to the sentencing framework (see Roberts and Cole, 1999).

[15] Under the Commission's scheme, each offence would carry one of four presumptive dispositions – two custodial presumptions and two community presumptions (Canadian Sentencing Commission, 1987, p 311). If the presumption was in favour of custody, the guideline would contain a sentence length range. In addition, the guideline would provide sentencers with a great deal of additional information including the following:

- summaries of recent Court of Appeal judgements;
- summaries of recent empirical sentencing patterns;
- lists of relevant mitigating and aggravating factors.

[16] We do not discuss the Magistrates' Court Sentencing Guidelines here. However, these constitute a more structured model of sentencing guidance. The guidelines provide magistrates with a clear methodology to apply when determining sentence, as well as guidance regarding the nature of disposition that should be imposed.

[17] This point is amply illustrated by the robbery guideline. The least serious form of the offence 'includes the threat or use of minimal force and removal of property'; it carries a sentence range from a very short prison sentence to three years in custody. This is a very broad range of sentence for an offence description which implies a relatively narrow spectrum of conduct (that is, the use or threat of minimal force).

[18] The MPC was established to insulate policy decisions about the money supply – and thus demand for credit – from short-term political considerations (and to insulate politicians from the consequences of these decisions).

[19] Most people can come to terms with the fact that in other areas of social policy, such as health and social care, investment decisions have to take account of affordability – even when the outcomes directly affect the length and quality of people's lives.

[20] One possibility would be to place a five-year review on a statutory basis.

[21] And in any case, as discussed above, attempts in 2005/06 to secure baseline data from administrative records on sentencing practice in 2002 proved unworkable.

[22] See, for example, www.justice.gov.uk/docs/stats-prison-pop-aug07.pdf

[23] For research illustrations of this phenomenon the reader is directed to Hough and Roberts (1998) and Roberts and Hough (2005).

References

Ashworth, A. (2008) *A structured sentencing framework and sentencing commission: Response from Professor Andrew Ashworth*, University of Oxford.

Bottoms, A.E., Rex, S. and Robinson, G. (2004) *Alternatives to prison: Options for an insecure society*, Cullompton: Willan Publishing.

Canadian Sentencing Commission (1987) *Sentencing reform: A Canadian approach*, Ottawa: Supply and Services Canada.

Frase, R. (2000) 'Is guided discretion sufficient? Overview of state sentencing guidelines', *Saint Louis University Law Journal*, vol 44, pp 425–46.

Frase, R. (2005a) 'State sentencing guidelines: Diversity, consensus, and unresolved policy issues', *Columbia Law Review*, vol 105, no 4, pp 1190–232.

Frase, R. (2005b) 'Sentencing guidelines in Minnesota', in M. Tonry (ed) *Crime and justice: A review of research*, Chicago: University of Chicago Press.

Gertner, N. (2008) 'The failures of the United States Sentencing Commission', in A. Freiberg, and K. Gelb (eds) *Penal populism, sentencing councils and sentencing policy*, Cullompton: Willan.

Hirst, M. (2008) 'Causing death by driving and other offences: A question of balance', *Criminal Law Review*, issue 5, May, pp 339–52.

Hough, M. and Jacobson, J. (2008) *Creating a sentencing commission for England and Wales: An opportunity to address the prisons crisis*, London: Prison Reform Trust.

Hough, M. and Roberts, J.V. (1998) *Attitudes to punishment: Findings from the British crime survey*, Home Office Research Study No. 179, London: Home Office.

Hough, M., Jacobson, J. and Millie, A. (2003) *The decision to imprison: Sentencing and the prison population*, London: Prison Reform Trust.

Hunt, K. and Connelly, M. (2005) 'Advisory guidelines in the post-Blakely era', *Federal Sentencing Reporter*, vol 17, no 4, pp 233-42.

Kauder, N., Ostrom, B., Peterson, M. and Rottman, D. (1997) *Sentencing commission profiles: State sentencing policy and practice research in action partnership*, Washington, DC: National Institute of Justice.

Lacey, N. (2008) *The prisoners' dilemma: Political economy and punishment in contemporary democracies*, Cambridge: Cambridge University Press.

Law Commission of New Zealand (2006) *Sentencing guidelines and parole reform*, Wellington: Law Commission of New Zealand, www.lawcom.govt.nz

Minnesota Sentencing Guidelines Commission (2007) *Minnesota sentencing guidelines and commentary*, revised 1 August 2007, www.msgc.state.mn.us/msgc5/guidelines.htm

Ostrom, B.J., Ostrom, C.W., Hanson, R.A. and Kleiman, M. (2008) *Assessing consistency and fairness in sentencing: A comparative study in three states*, Williamsburg, VA: National Center for State Courts, www.ncsconline.org/images/PEWExecutiveSummaryv10.pdf

Reitz, K.R. (2005) 'The new sentencing conundrum: policy and constitutional law at cross-purposes', *Columbia Law Review*, vol 105, no 4, pp 1083–123.

Roberts, J.V. (2008) *Punishing persistent offenders*, Oxford: Oxford University Press.

Roberts, J.V. and Cole, D. (eds) (1999) *Making sense of sentencing*, Toronto: University of Toronto Press.

Roberts, J.V. and Hough, M. (2005) *Understanding public attitudes to criminal justice*, Maidenhead: Open University Press.

Roberts, J.V., Hough, M., Jacobson, J., Bredee, A. and Moon, N. (2008) 'Public attitudes to sentencing offenders convicted of offences involving death by driving', *Criminal Law Review*, issue 7, July, pp 525–40.

Sentencing Commission for Scotland (2006) *Sentencing guidelines around the world*, Edinburgh: Sentencing Commission for Scotland.

Sentencing Commission Working Group (2008a) *A structured sentencing framework and sentencing commission: A consultation paper*, London: Ministry of Justice.

Sentencing Commission Working Group (2008b) *Sentencing guidelines in England and Wales: An evolutionary approach*, London: Ministry of Justice.

Sentencing Commission Working Group (2008c) *A summary of responses to the Sentencing Commission Working Group's consultation paper*, London: Ministry of Justice.

Spelman, W. (2005) 'Jobs or jails: The crime drop in Texas', *Journal of Policy Analysis and Management*, vol 24, no 1, pp 133–65.

Tonry, M. (1996) *Sentencing matters*, New York: Oxford University Press.

von Hirsch, A., Bottoms, A.E., Burney, E. and Wikström, P-O. (1999) *Criminal deterrence and sentencing severity: An analysis of recent research*, Oxford: Hart Publishing.

Wolff, M. (2006) Missouri's information-based discretionary sentencing system, *Ohio State Journal of Criminal Law*, vol 4, no 1, pp 95–120.

Young, W. (2008) Sentencing reform in New Zealand: A proposal to establish a sentencing council', in A. Freiberg and K. Gelb (eds) *Penal populism, sentencing councils and sentencing policy*, Cullompton: Willan Publishing.

Young, W. and Browning, C. (2008) 'New Zealand's sentencing council', *Criminal Law Review*, issue 4, April, pp 287–98.

'Titan' prisons: do size, efficiency and legitimacy matter?

5

Alison Liebling

> Effective management of the prison system is critical to the integrity of the criminal justice system as a whole. (Carter, 2007, p 3)

> When you are working in a prison, you can see how easily it could all slip away from you … (Senior manager, personal communication, 2008)

> These prisons will not be prisoner warehouses. (Prison Service, 2007, p 1)

> The Review's vision is for a prison system which encourages innovation, efficiency and competition but with a clear line of accountability from the prisons minister to prison officer. The structure and focus of the prison system should, over time, be reconfigured to increase the focus on both service delivery and offender management. (Carter, 2007, p 3)

The Carter Report 2007

Lord Carter's Report was commissioned to explore ways of saving money, and building new capacity. Since size is a major determinant of cost, considerable thought has been devoted to the question of what the 'optimal' size of a new prison might be. The report recommends the building of two to three 'larger, state of the art' or 'Titan' prisons accommodating around 2,500 prisoners each. The term is objectionable, referring to giant stature and physical strength or power (The New Shorter Oxford Dictionary, 1994) so I wonder whether we should refer to them more descriptively and neutrally, as the large, cluster concept. These prisons should be 'planned and developed now so that from 2012 there can be approximately 5,000 new places that will allow for a programme of closures of old, inefficient, and ineffective prisons offering better value for money and much improved chances of reducing re-offending and crime' (Carter, 2007, p 1). Carter's Report, we should note, is given the sub-title, 'Proposals for the efficient and sustainable use of custody in England and Wales', not 'Proposals for the legitimate use of custody in England and Wales'. His task was 'to consider options for improving the balance between the supply of prison places and demand for them' (Carter, 2007, p 1). The Titan or large, multifunctional prison concept is all about cost effectiveness. It might be interesting to think through how the report might have looked different had the concept of legitimacy been part of the agenda.[1]

Members of the Working Group argue that while, in an ideal world, 'we would not be operating a Titan', size is never mentioned as a significant factor impacting on quality or performance in inspectorate reports. What matters, according to Carter, are staff culture, management processes, buildings and crowding. Aspects of existing practice are not ideal, and 'we are not living in an ideal world' (Member of the Carter Working Group, personal communication, 2008). This commentator suggested that 'smaller communities, or prisons of around 400 prisoners, are more successful but about four times more expensive'. This is 'not feasible in the current political climate', or acceptable to the contemporary taxpayer.

This efficiency-utilitarian position is the strongest concern I have with the strategy. Let me declare a position: I prefer Rousseau to Hobbes, Rawls to Nozick, and social democracy to Conservative neo-liberalism.[2] I chose the Cambridge college I applied for when starting my PhD on the basis of its size, with age and beauty coming second. I might be a 'utopian realist', that is, someone who adheres to a political version of appreciative inquiry, where a better future is created out of real current trends (see Giddens 1998, 1990 and also Loader, 1998[3]). These value positions inevitably influence my response to the proposals. I am also influenced by 20 years of prisons research experience. Swansea prison, which housed 366 prisoners in old and expensive accommodation in a research study conducted in 2002–04 (it was built in 1861), had the major advantage that it was staffed disproportionately by local people, and prisoners accommodated there were not too far away from their homes. It was a high-risk prison with fewer than the expected number of suicides, given its population. It also had good staff–prisoner relationships, and was described as unusually safe by prisoners. They 'trusted in the environment' and felt that staff cared about them, for example on entry into custody (Liebling et al, 2005). I wonder if the review team should have done more searching of the evidence on size and quality or outcomes, since the data are easily available. Swansea was the smallest prison of 12 we included in a recent study of suicide prevention and it was better on almost all measures of moral performance than any other prison in the study, despite its dilapidated (and therefore expensive) buildings. The other small prison in the study, Eastwood Park, was successfully improved by a performance test process as well as being the most successful implementer of the new suicide prevention strategy. It is possible, then, that small is beautiful – or at least less cumbersome, complex and resistant. I shall return to this possibility below.

The three new Titan prisons would consist of five self-contained units holding approximately 500 offenders in each.[4] They would 'draw on best practice in the existing estate to introduce first-class, efficient working practices from the outset, ensuring that regime and facilities are available to provide satisfactory opportunities for purposeful activities, such as employment and training' (Caret, 2007, p 38). Their design would incorporate optimal sight lines, centralised support services, and new technology built into the fabric.

They will be built where need is greatest: in London, the West Midlands, and the North West. It is assumed that they will house adult males. The 'operational challenges' associated with large prisons include the possibility of large-scale disturbances, difficulties in meeting the needs of specific groups of prisoners, or managing prisoners of different types on the same site, and the 'management complexities associated with a large staff complement'.

The Isle of Sheppey cluster currently houses 2,224 prisoners and is expected to house a new houseblock shortly, so with or without Titan prisons, scale is increasing to around this size.[5] The main rationale for moving upwards in size, overtly acknowledged by all, is economies of scale rather than prison management philosophy. There is also a widespread consensus that most existing old Victorian local prisons 'need reinventing' (personal communication, 2008). The clustering process has not yet been satisfactorily achieved, so the Prison Service is still learning about the complexities of shared services, facilities, and multiple function sites. The proposed time scale for the acquisition of land, building and opening of the first Titan prison is four to five years. The claim being made is that this 'should improve the prisoner experience' (personal communication, 2008). Concerns discussed by the Workgroup include 'management grip, order and control, and the (distinctive, tight) style of governing necessary to successfully manage this kind of establishment' (personal communication, 2008):

> Our strategy is to have our best people, the best processes, to get it right, initially ... we need more evidence on what works and what doesn't work in running prisons. The argument against Titans is that they will be too big to manage. (personal communication, 2008)

The three private companies consulted said that the model was workable.[6] It will require 'more flexibility among staff, without threatening staff–prisoner relationships'.

Alongside Carter's recommendations relating to Titan prisons, there are calls for measures to 'moderate the use of custody' by 2014, and to modernise (that is, lower the cost of) the prison by reducing the cost of the workforce, supported by a market testing of the new capacity. So we have new, large prisons, an assumption that there will be competition to run them, and a plan to reduce the 'costly, outdated and inflexible pay and grading structure' currently applied to prison officers. There are good reasons to be pursuing this agenda, and legitimate reasons to be considering the role, pay and professional standing of prison officers. But it is not clear what the right answers are, or what rationale is driving these changes. There is talk of 'modest' sentence control and of eventually closing some of the older and more inefficient prisons, if all this works. Again, there are some good arguments for doing this. Lord Carter's report on prisons, *Managing offenders, reducing crime* (2003) was also intended to reduce the use of custody. His track record, then, is less than impressive. The main thrust of his argument in his latest report (Carter, 2007) is that penal capacity should be reconciled with current criminal justice policy.

Scholars of the prison have used a wide range of language with which to talk about the use of imprisonment. Nils Christie refers to the 'carceral texture' of society, arguing that prison population size is a policy choice (Christie, 1993). We should remember that examples exist of deliberate and successful decarceration (Finland, and what was then West Germany). David Downes talked of the 'depth of imprisonment' when comparing penal policy in the Netherlands with that of England and Wales (Downes, 1988). Attitudes towards, and practices relating to, normalisation, welfare, discipline, punishment and rehabilitation, the role of prison staff, and rights and privileges including home leave and visits, impact on how psychologically invasive and damaging prison sentences are. These attitudes and practices differ between jurisdictions in ways that are indicative of visions of the offender and broader social and cultural relations. Roy King and Kathleen McDermott talked later of the 'weight' or psychological burden of a prison sentence, reserving the term 'depth' for practices relating to security and control (King and McDermott, 1995). Their preferred term, 'weight', included material conditions, rights and privileges, and the nature and quality of staff–prisoner relationships. These differ between jurisdictions but also between prisons within a jurisdiction, in a way reminiscent of the Measuring the Quality of Prison Life (MQPL) findings.[7] Recently Ben Crewe has referred to the increasing 'grip' or 'tightness' of imprisonment, as prisoners are required to actively engage with the complex requirements of new sentences (Crewe, 2008). David Garland referred to this phenomenon as 'responsibilisation'. On all measures, then, quantity, depth, weight and tightness, the prison has grown and deepened in England and Wales since the early 1990s (Liebling, 2004). We are the highest user of imprisonment in Western Europe, and hold more life sentenced prisoners than all of the rest of Western Europe put together.

We need to conceptually separate concerns about increasing prison use, from the need for newly designed prison facilities, and from the case for large new prison facilities. It is theoretically possible to argue both for medium sized new-build prisons and for decarceration (or penal restraint). There is also a policy question deserving of thorough discussion and empirical examination about the use of the private sector to run Titan prisons. The evidence base on relative quality, performance or outcomes is thin, to date. There may well be a case for the replacement of old prisons with new facilities. Governors argue that dilapidated, Victorian, prisons are 'almost unmanageable'. Other jurisdictions, such as Western Australia and some American states, having adopted our Victorian designs, have closed their oldest prisons and turned them into museums. There is a need for something better than police cells or the unsatisfactory buildings of Brixton, and new prisons offer the opportunity to experiment with potentially better design and facilities. New prisons have several advantages, including: the chance to establish a specific ideology or culture, to design in safety, to unite staff around positive goals and to take advantage of new thinking about first night centres, and to locate prisoners closer to home. New prisons are notoriously difficult to open, however, so attention needs to be paid to ways of accomplishing stability in the early years.

I want to consider four issues in this paper. First, a review of some of the problems faced by contemporary prisons and to what extent the case exists for new-build establishments. Second, the question of prison size and its effects on prison life. Third, I want to raise several 'missing problems' for policy and implementation teams, as well as interested critics, to consider. Finally, I will summarise with some thoughts about the Carter Report more generally and its approach to the problems faced by the Prison Service.

Problems faced by contemporary prisons in England and Wales include overcrowding and unpredictable population growth, the need to control costs, expensive and unsuitable accommodation, prisoners located in the wrong parts of the country far away from their homes, high levels of risk of disorder and suicide, cultural resistance to change and, in some cases, care for prisoners among staff, industrial unrest, and poor outcomes. There is continuing uncertainty about what is required of the contemporary prison: safe care, drug treatment, punishment, containment or future crime prevention.[8] There is increasing and often incoherent political use made of whimsical penal strategies, which often have far-reaching effects on the tricky business of getting through the day peacefully. A strategy is needed that will address all of these problems. New-build prisons would be helpful, under the right circumstances.

There are also some 'essential features' of British prisons which are enduring and which emerge continually in research. One of these is that staff identify strongly with their landing or houseblock and also very powerfully with 'their prison'. They have faith in 'what worked yesterday', but are perturbed by future-oriented reorganisations of their work, and they need to feel safe in order to care for prisoners (Liebling and Price, 2001). Prisons are special, place-based communities whose form is shaped by social and political ideas held about crime, punishment, social order and human nature. They suffer from an 'inherent legitimacy deficit' (Sparks, 1994) and are susceptible to brutality, indifference to human needs, abuses of power and breakdowns in order. Prison staff are difficult to manage, and engage in 'low visibility work'. Prisons pose daily moral and management problems, and getting thorough the day peacefully is a difficult and contingent task which has to be continually worked at. Staff and prisoners frequently express the need to be individually known. Highly competent governors capable of leading and motivating staff, keeping an eye on the detail, orchestrating an effective senior management team, of ensuring that sometimes competing targets are reached in ways that make sense, and who manage to be visible to staff, are in short supply. This brief review of the problems faced by prisons constitutes a critical case for reform.

The relationship between prison size and quality

Lord Woolf argued in his detailed analysis of the prison system in England and Wales that the optimal size for a prison was 400 prisoners (Home Office, 1991). He said:

The first principle is that normally prisoners should be accommodated in prison units of approximately 50/70 prisoners. The prison itself should not normally hold more than 400 prisoners ... The evidence suggests that if these figures are exceeded, there can be a marked fall off in all aspects of the performance of a prison ... Prisons and units established in accordance with the figures which we have recommended should enable good relations to be maintained between staff and inmates, a constructive regime to be provided, and proper and effective management of the prison as a whole to be maintained, at a realistic cost. (Home Office 1991, p 266)

Woolf referred to a Prison Service Design Briefing (PSDB) published in 1988 aimed at bringing together 'existing guidance and instructions relating to prison design and construction'. The inquiry received evidence from 'a distinguished panel of architects on behalf of the Royal Institute of British Architects'. Woolf said:

The PSDB proposals are based on a prison having a capacity for 600 prisoners, divided into groups of between 40 to 60, with a group of 50 providing a good balance. The PSDB describes the figure of 600 as being 'the optimum balance between the need for effective relationships and control of prisoners and economies of scale'. The total of 600 within a prison is a higher number than we regard as ideal. However, a prison of 600 prisoners can be operated as two prisons. This is what we would like to see happen if a prison is designed to hold that number. (Home Office 1991, p 267)

Several analyses of prison life and quality provide empirical support for the argument that 'small is better'. A prison quality study conducted in Norway by Johnsen and colleagues in all 32 high security prisons (of 50 establishments in total) using a translated version of the MQPL and SQL questionnaires[9] found that despite longer and more elaborate training for prison staff, prisoner evaluations of staff–prisoner relationships and their treatment more generally were similar to evaluations by prisoners in England and Wales, with significant differences (within a fairly narrow range) between establishments of similar types. Staff tended to evaluate relationships more positively than prisoners did, except in those establishments where prisoner ratings were highest (Johnsen et al, 2008).[10] These establishments were characterised by a consensus between staff and prisoners on prisoners' quality of life. The prisons included in the study ranged in size from 392 to 12 prisoners. The authors analysed the data in three groups, by prison size. Small prisons were defined as those prisons with less than 50 prisoners (n = 20); medium-sized prisons were those with 50 to 100 prisoners (n = 5) and large prisons held more than 100 prisoners (n = 7).

Significantly higher scores were found at the smallest prisons on eight of the 14 staff quality of life dimensions compared with the largest prisons. The largest difference was on the dimension 'Attitude towards senior management' (3.39 in small prisons, 3.18 in medium-sized prisons and 2.72 in large prisons). The differences between small and large prisons were even clearer in prisoner evaluations of the quality of their lives in prison (Table 5.1). These mean scores are based on 274 prisoners in small

Table 5.1: Dimension scores for prisoners

	Prison size		
	Small <50	Medium 50–100	Large >100
Relationships with staff*	3.47	2.89	2.82
Overall treatment*	3.31	2.88	2.72
Well being*	3.15	2.77	2.62
Personal safety*	3.70	3.47	3.30
Personal development*	2.71	2.36	2.29
Respect*	3.01	2.55	2.46
Decency*	3.32	3.01	3.08
Entry into custody*	2.97	2.66	2.59
Order and organisation*	3.34	2.95	2.85
Fairness*	2.95	2.71	2.62
Race equality*	3.52	3.18	3.19
Family contact*	2.79	2.35	2.37
Support for personal safety*	3.25	2.93	2.87
Offending behaviour courses	2.99	3.08	2.83
Specialist care/care for those at risk*	2.68	2.51	2.35
Healthcare	2.71	2.61	2.72

Note: * These dimensions had a significantly higher score ($p < 0.05$) at small prisons (<50), compared with large prisons (>100).

prisons, 194 prisoners in medium-sized prisons and 664 prisoners in large prisons (total sample 1,132 prisoners).

The dimension scores on staff–prisoner relationships were 3.47 in small prisons, 2.89 in medium-sized prisons and 2.82 in large prisons (on a 5 point scale where 3 is a neutral evaluation and lower scores are negative, higher scores are positive). The differences between the large and small prison scores were statistically significant, on all but two dimensions. Small prisons offer few offending behaviour courses, and the dimension 'healthcare' tends to be rated poorly everywhere. Better 'moral performance' (in my language) was found in smaller prisons.

A report published in 2006 by Hammerlin and Mathiassen, based on qualitative interviews with prison staff and prisoners in Norway, also showed that small prisons had certain advantages: because of the small number of prisoners that prison officers had to attend to, the relationship between prison officers and prisoners was closer in these prisons (Hammerlin and Mathiassen, 2006). Small prisons were more 'transparent' and 'prison officers knew the prisoners and what to expect of them'. They could therefore be more sensitive to changes in attitudes among prisoners. They could react quickly when prisoners had problems and could respond more effectively to their needs. The communication lines between staff and senior managers were shorter and consequently information was exchanged quickly and decisions were made more speedily. The organisation was more flexible and dynamic, because there was less bureaucracy and a closer relationship between different levels in the organisation. Prison officers in small prisons had a less monotonous job than their colleagues in larger prisons where working tasks tended to be more specialised. However, Hammerlin and Mathiassen also argued that staff working in small prisons had to be 'more aware of their professional role': that is, that professional boundaries could sometimes be breached. This problem – of reconciling close relationships with professional boundaries – has been found in other studies of very small units (Bottomley et al, 1994).

Johnsen et al concluded that 'small prisons have a better climate than larger prisons' (Johnsen et al, 2008). This kind of analysis should be replicated in England and Wales.[11] Straightforward analyses of important 'quality' indicators (assaults, suicides, self-harm, use of control and restraint and so on) by prison size would be relatively easy to carry out using officially recorded data.

Some missing problems

There are six areas where problems arise which are deserving of discussion but not acknowledged in the Carter Report. These are:

1. the risks inherent in the concept of efficiency;
2. the future-orientation of Service Level Agreements (SLAs);
3. problems of 'interior legitimacy';
4. the operationalisation of the large, cluster prison concept;
5. the assumption that women 'need smaller units';
6. problems of 'exterior legitimacy'.

I shall address each of these problems briefly below.

The risks inherent in the concept of efficiency

The case for Titan prisons casts them as a legitimate outcome of contemporary fiscal and social circumstances. The new 'estates policy' reflects concern with the control of expenditure, and a boundary-drawing, 'them/us' model of offending. But previous analyses have shown that the concept of efficiency is 'ethically blind'. American scholars Feeley and Simon identified an 'emerging constellation of discourses and practices, knowledge and power' known as 'actuarial justice' in the 1990s, which promotes the concept of efficiency and provides a rationale for it. Actuarial models of justice risk neglecting the moral agency of persons (Feeley and Simon, 1992). They prioritise the identification, classification, incapacitation and management of unruly risk groups rather than the understanding or handling of them as moral, psychological or economic agents. According to Feeley and Simon, actuarial justice invites new forms of custody and surveillance, including 'no frills' varieties of prison use and high parole revocation rates (Feeley and Simon, 1994). It emphasises utilitarian purposes over moral considerations.

We need to be very wary of a preoccupation with efficiency ('feasibility and cost', pp 15–16) that brings in its wake moral indifference. There are of course good moral arguments for being careful with and held accountable for public expenditure. But general questions of value have come to be *replaced*, rather than *restrained*, by questions of technical efficacy (Garland, 1990, p 7). Bureaucracy and its framing of problems in a technicist language, geared towards the twin (internal) goals of efficiency and efficacy, 'kills' morality (Boutellier, 2001; see also Daems, 2008, p 155). There can be a sinister edge to large, efficient, bureaucratic organisations, which can become impersonal or, at worst, horrifying (see Bauman, 1992).[12] The question of what kind of institutions, indeed prisons, we design shapes the state of our society, civilisation and culture. They are likely to become not exceptions but the new norm.[13] The warning we should heed, already noted by classic prison scholars, is that large bureaucratic institutions tend to displace external goals with internal, self-maintenance purposes: internal order and security are prioritised over any rehabilitative aspirations. Richard Sennett has provided a persuasive analysis of the speeded up 'new economy' and its threats to institutional loyalty, informal trust, and the build-up of institutional knowledge (Sennett, 2006). These themes will recur later in this chapter. In the new economy, he argues, politicians behave like consumers rather than craftsmen. They lack direction and commitment, favouring consultants, and working to a shortened time-frame. Institutional life becomes superficial. These are dangers we should heed. As well as innovation, employees need a 'mental and emotional anchor; they need values which assess whether changes in work … are worthwhile' (Sennett 2006, p 185). Without such an anchor, some form of revolt against the new economic imperative and its 'fragile politics' is likely (p 197). Efficiency is *one* important value. It should be balanced against others, like the building and safeguarding of just institutions.

The future-orientation of SLAs

The Titan concept is about more than the question of size. Modern management is also eager to, in the words of one governor of an SLA prison, 'see if I could deliver against the book of promises'. Service Level Agreements are, like private prison contracts, a new tool in prison management, with little evidence available as yet about their quality, operation in practice or effects. That the private sector find 'these contract arrangements to be well managed and effective' is one measure of the power of contracts to secure accountability and decent services. But these questions should be answered independently, and with explicit criteria; for example, are prisoners prepared for release more effectively when a prison runs to a contract or SLA? Carter's comments on efficiencies and modernisation are based on a paper analysis of the original Blakenhurst Service Level Agreement. It is widely known that the cost of running Blakenhurst is significantly more than planned in the original contract. The Carter team report that 'locating and validating the cost for HMP Blakenhurst has proved time-consuming' but that efficiencies can be made. The assumption in the report, then, is that the Blakenhurst SLA was appropriate, but that inappropriate drift has occurred, typical of the public sector. Other analyses of the Blakenhurst SLA (by members of the bid team) suggest that there were unintended consequences of bidding for a prison in a highly competitive environment (see Liebling, 2004, pp 104–6). There is a sociological reality to the bidding process, which can mean that unrealistic promises are made. Corners are cut, resourcing is impossibly tight, and the prison may prove impossible to run once the contract has been signed. Different accounts are available of the history of Blakenhurst, and it is a pity that close evaluation and documentation of the effectiveness of these new management practices have not been carried out.

The Carter Review recommends an 'aggressive programme of cost and activity profiling across the public sector estate' resulting in an 'efficient cost' for each prison (p 36). It is clear that the financial management of prisons is going to become much tighter. The Titan model is not just big, but big and cheap ('the Tesco model'). There is much talk in the report of market testing at least some of these SLAs (for example, where there is any disagreement about the efficient cost) before making decisions. Governors are expressing concern about the search for cost savings being too savage. There is an important distinction to be made between reducing inefficiencies and doing business on the cheap. Prison staff turnover is low in public sector prisons and high in private sector prisons: what does this tell us and where is the optimum rate? Conversations about whether prison officers receive enough training for their increasingly complex role continue to raise the question of cost: 'If we provided more professional training, we would have to pay them more.' These are moral as well as policy choices. Imprisoning less rather than more cheaply is one alternative policy option.

In a briefing document prepared by the Prison Service, it is 'anticipated that the Titan regime will continue to focus on the strong dynamic interaction between officers and prisoners. This will ensure that specific needs of individual prisoners are continually assessed and decency standards are maintained' (p 1). This is a promise, and one we should watch closely. More and larger prisons means more prison staff recruitment and training. Addressing the 'costly, outdated and inflexible pay and grading structure that currently exists' in the public sector is important, but we should also look closely at whether staff working in the private sector are too loosely bonded to their organisations and whether an unintended price is being paid for cheaper, high turnover labour (see Liebling and Crewe, in progress). Staff cannot easily be deployed in several areas at once, without losses in trust, relationships more generally, and expertise. Flexibility comes at a price.

Problems of interior legitimacy

On publication of the first Carter Report, and the 2001 Criminal Justice Act, critics observed that prisons were being constructed in the public and policy imagination as simply 'places of punishment and service delivery', where offending behaviour work started in them could be followed up on release into the community (for example, in the custody plus sentence). Such a vision omits two decades of research and scholarly analysis (as well as senior practitioner commentary) suggesting that prisons are inherently complex, morally dangerous, and unstable institutions, with other less obvious or instrumental purposes besides reducing reoffending, such as the expression of public rage, the demarcation of moral boundaries, the realisation of political authority, and the shaping of values (see, for example, Garland, 1990). Prisons differ, their cultures range from constructive and pro-social to indifferent or, at worst, brutal. To forget that prisons suffer from an inherent legitimacy deficit, that order has to be worked at, or that their moral performance differs significantly is to invite catastrophe. As Woolf argued in 1991, prisoners have legitimate expectations of certain standards of treatment, including fairness, openness in decision making and respect. Very few prisons meet high standards of legitimacy, and most establishments suffer from 'value imbalance' of one kind or another. Our understanding of what makes prisons more rather than less legitimate, the role of culture, management, and values in shaping this equation, and the possible links between 'interior legitimacy' and prisoners' well-being or other important outcomes, has only just begun (see, for example, Liebling, 2004; Drake, 2007; Tait, 2008). Larger prisons, with highly competent but remote governors (or chief executives) may make the struggle for legitimate regimes and staff behaviour harder.

Operationalisation of the large, cluster prison concept

Questions of location, design and operation are yet to be decided. Evidence to date suggests that cheap builds are not successful. A prison's location determines the impact on prisoners' families, via distance and accessibility, but also the recruitment, quality and turnover of prison staff and specialists. One of the differences between prisons operated by the private sector in performance over time is related to surrounding economic conditions. Where employment levels are high and pay is relatively good, it is more difficult to recruit and retain staff. High turnover leads to continued lack of experience and frustrations for existing staff, which tends to lower morale, performance and efficiency. Decisions will need to be taken about management and organisation. If the prison is very large, would the governing governor 'govern', or would there be five more junior (less experienced) governors, overseen by a chief executive? Given the increasing complexities of prison management (Jacobs and Olitsky, 2004), and the importance to staff of senior management visibility, it would be a mistake to govern from a distance. Laming said, in his 2001 report, *Modernising the Management of the Prison Service*, that, 'to succeed Governors must know exactly what is going on in their prison' (Home Office, 2001, p 25). Prison officer work is inherently 'low visibility' work, in need of strong, clear direction and leadership. The longer the management chain and the more distant the top figure, the more difficult it will be to send the right signals to staff, or to shape staff culture at wing level. Do we know enough about what good practice looks like, and what shapes it, to know what a legitimate 'Carter prison' would look like in practice?[14] There exists a maturing body of private sector competition, but there is little organised reflection at the top of the organisation concerning what lessons have been learned about the strengths and weaknesses of each sector in managing staff, quality or outcomes. A public consultation is being held on these and related matters as we complete our contributions to this book (Ministry of Justice, 2008). One of the characteristics of better quality prisons we have found in several studies is high levels of trust, particularly between staff and senior managers (Liebling, 2004; Liebling et al, 2005; Gadd and Shefer, 2006). This is often related to management visibility as well as competence. The concept of trust is asymmetric, in the sense that it grows slowly but can be lost in an instant; it is positively related to dignity and respect, and to individual recognition. Where it grows, it becomes a 'lubricant of social co-operation' (Sztompka, 1999, p 62). The presence and flow of trust is therefore an important quality in any organisation. In prisons, like communication, it is especially difficult to generate and is normally at low levels. A strategy would be needed to ensure better than typical levels of both communication and trust in prisons of a very large size. This will be difficult in prisons where 'number one governors' are somewhat remote.

The assumption that women 'need smaller units'

It is often the case that women prisoners are treated as 'different and special' with distinct needs and circumstances. It is explicitly stated in the Carter Report that Titan prisons may suit men but not women. Why is this? What does this imply about men and the male prison population (and on the basis of what evidence)? The empirical evidence suggests that the adult male prison population has within it a subgroup of highly vulnerable, sexually abused, psychiatrically fragile men with complex family roles who match women prisoners on risk of suicide and need for support (see for example, Liebling, 1999). It is not always obvious who such prisoners are. To dismiss the male population as somehow amenable to more distant and impersonal management is naïve and discriminatory. If there is an argument for keeping women out of Titan prisons, I would like to see it fully articulated, next to the detailed case for housing men in them, in the light of these arguments made for women. Observers have noticed the stark contrast between the proposals in the Corston Report for women, which link criminal justice with social policy (Corston, 2007), and the proposals by Lord Carter – 'for men'. Far fewer of the Corston proposals have been accepted, but it is lazy logic to suggest that a new (and far from ideal) socially narrowed strategy for penal policy is better reserved for men.

Problems of exterior legitimacy

Prisoners are beginning to express hopelessness and frustration with longer and more arduous sentences, which are difficult to manage one's way through. The requirements placed on prisoners to obtain declassification, parole and home leave, are increasingly stringent (and in many cases, unobtainable). As Richard Sparks argues in his article, 'Can Prisons be Legitimate?' there is a complex interplay between the material (I would add, emotional and moral) conditions of prison life, and the external, ideological, structural and economic conditions in which such prisons exist (Sparks, 1994). Increasing sentence lengths, a harshening climate, and continued population growth make the prison experience feel less legitimate in the eyes of prisoners, even if the interior conditions are reasonable. Questions of exterior legitimacy include the fairness and transparency of policy decision making (including any bidding process), accountability and the extent of democratic deliberation involved in such decision making. A major problem with Titan prisons is that these important matters have so far been largely evaded. Sparks argues that 'all penal discourse can be scrutinized … in terms of its orientation towards legitimation problems' (Sparks, 1994, p 20). Current penal discourse has apparently swept the concept of legitimacy under the carpet, privileging 'economic efficiency' over morality. The combined effects of this new 'economic rationalism' (Pusey, 1992) with a reemerging 'scientism' and unrestrained punitiveness in public and political thinking about offenders is 'altering the contours of the penal realm' (Sparks, 1994, p 24) in ways that are deeply troubling.

Conclusion

The Carter Report ends by reminding us that the rise in the size of the prison population since 1945 has been constant and steady:

> There is therefore a need for a focussed and informed public debate about penal policy. It will be important to consider whether to continue to have one of the largest prison populations per capita in the world and to devote increasing sums of public expenditure to building and running prisons and responding to fluctuating pressures as they emerge. Not only is it costly, inefficient and a demand on scarce land, but the sporadic way in which the pressures emerge and are responded to inhibits the delivery of effective offender management and rehabilitation. (Carter, 2007, p 30)

Many commentators would prefer to see a thorough and well-informed reevaluation of the role of the prison, and a diversion of these funds into 'justice reinvestment'. How problems are defined limits the dialogue or possibilities of authentic communication and then policies are crafted out of these limited rationalities. More prison, achieved cheaply, is one policy option but it fails to take account of David Garland's critique that the prison is a 'tragic' option, beset by irresolvable tensions and symbolising broken social relations. The 'conditions which do most to induce conformity ... lie outside the jurisdiction of penal institutions' (Garland, 1990, p 289). Even if we were to agree that new prisons, with better designs, are desirable, in opting for large clusters the Carter proposals are privileging a certain economic kind of understanding of the problems faced. We risk forgetting there are other shared aims (such as social justice, crime prevention and inclusion, or legitimate prison communities) and there is a moral language which has been excluded from this debate (an 'instrumental rationality' dominates; see Dryzek, 1995). What does it mean for us socially, morally and politically when the main determinant of policy is the loaded and now frequently used term, 'we have to be realistic'?[15] There are different visions of what is realistic. I come back to a distinction we may wish to pursue further between utopian realism and cynical or pragmatic realism. Jonathan Sacks and Hans Boutellier both remind us there are meant to be limits to legal sanctions – they put 'seal on the wax of moral sentiments'. In other words, methods of social control should be embedded in social arrangements, with the law only stepping in at the margins (Boutellier, 2001). We are placing the law centre stage, and it simply cannot do, nor was it ever intended to do, this amount of work. What we are seeing is the politics of fear overriding the politics of hope (Sacks, 2000). Large prisons pose risks.

If they go ahead, as I suspect they will, then their design and opening should be closely managed in a way that takes full account of what is already known about the problems of opening new prisons, the difficulties of establishing pro-social or positive cultures in new prisons while maintaining order, and the new problems of scale, with all the management challenges this will pose. More attention should be paid to the question of what form a cluster might take if it were to have penal and moral (as well as fiscal) legitimacy. They should adhere to a well-resourced offender management model, so that offenders are housed, prepared for release, and then released, as close as possible to their home areas. They should be carefully and independently evaluated against the promises made in the report about best practice, outcomes, and substitution for smaller establishments, and also against our best understanding of standards of interior and exterior legitimacy. They should not provide us with an excuse to avoid in the medium term the very real problems of overuse of the prison in England and Wales and the likely long-term legitimation problems we will face as a result.

Notes

[1] There is a feeling that the Prison Service was treated generously in the past, with high expectations about the returns on this additional investment in programmes and regimes. These expectations (which were not directly about legitimacy either) have not been met.

[2] That is, I prefer social policies supporting greater inclusion, social justice and equality (see Giddens, 1998).

[3] Loader argues that 'a utopian realist criminological stance endeavours to connect issues of crime and social regulation with questions of ethics and politics, and enter the public conversation about crime equipped with an articulated, principled and future-oriented set of normative values and political objectives (the utopianism). But it also seeks to engage with the *realpolitik* of crime and criminal justice, and formulate (for example, crime reduction) proposals that have some immanent purchase on the world (the realism)'. Utopian realism is 'systematic', 'normative in orientation', and 'prudent' as opposed to instrumental and technical. It never loses sight of 'the intimate connection between crime, politics and ethics' (Loader, 1998, p 207).

[4] But with two segregation units of 50 prisoners each, according to the outline design brief.

[5] Clusters are under development on the Isle of Wight (1,617) and in Redditch (1,427).

[6] Others consulted during the process included area managers, governors and members of the Prisons Board. As is often the case in the policy-making process (see Rock, 1995), there has not been universal support within the Prison Service of the Ministry of Justice for the concept. The Chief Inspector of Prisons, the Prison Reform Trust and the International Centre for Prison Studies are opposed to the proposals.

[7] Surveys on the 'moral performance' or inner quality of life of prisoners, as evaluated by prisoners (see Liebling, 2004).

[8] In the language of the report, 'Challenging the efficiency of public sector prisons is difficult, as a clear view of the desired output and outcomes of prison is lacking as well as how much this should cost' (p 22).

[9] Measuring the Quality of Prison Life and Staff Quality of Life, respectively; see Liebling (2004), Gadd and Shefer (2006), Arnold et al (2007).

[10] The research was conducted by Berit Johnsen, Per Kristian Granheim and Janne Helgesen in 2007–08. Questionnaires (used and translated with our permission) were returned by 1,078 officers and 1,132 prisoners, response rates of 44% and 55% respectively (see further Johnsen et al, 2008). For the following section I am most grateful to Berit Johnsen for sharing the data from this research, for discussions about her findings, and for her translations of the work conducted by Hammerlin and Mathiassen.

[11] Prompted by discussions arising from the Titan prison proposals, and Johnsen's findings, an analysis of MQPL data collected by Standards Audit Unit by prison size is

currently under way (Liebling and McLean, in progress). A first look at the data shows that smaller prisons are rated significantly more positively by prisoners.

[12] Bauman argues that atrocities can emerge in modern societies when old, unresolved tensions (such as fears and conflicts) meet the 'powerful instruments of rational and effective action that modern development itself brought into being' (Bauman, 1992, p xiv). His warning is that apparently civilised, modern, bureaucratic social and technological developments used for social engineering have hidden within them the potential to dehumanise as well as the potential to enhance life (pp 1–9). The Holocaust, he argues, 'was a legitimate resident in the house of modernity' (p 17). Modern bureaucracies have the ability 'to coordinate the action of a great number of moral individuals in the pursuit of any, also immoral, ends' (p 18). He reminds us, after Elias, that 'right policies' do not mean the elimination of human problems (p 12).

[13] As Bauman starkly warns us, it was budget balancing, means-ends calculus, and expert advice that led to a decision to exterminate rather than export the Jews (Bauman, 1992, pp 15–19).

[14] A discussion with Professor Richard Harding, Chief Inspector of Prisons in Western Australia, on a draft of this paper led to a series of reflections on what it would mean to 'do it properly' (where a consensus could be accomplished about what 'properly' means). Is the proposed model five distinct institutions on one loosely linked site (for example, a male Cat 'A', a male local prison, a young offender institution (YOI), a therapeutic community, and a female cross-category prison)? If that were the model, it would follow that inter-changeability of custodial staff would not be possible – unless this were restricted to gatehouse staff or recovery teams or other staff whose activities are neutral in cultural terms. 'Most of the staff would need to be trained for their particular tasks, and the only circumstance in which they could swap across prisons within the cluster would be after appropriate further training (or temporarily in some emergency situation). There may be an economy of scale with regard to health services and education staff. The overall running costs would still not be reduced in the way that Carter contemplates because the custodial staff savings would not occur. Each cluster would have to be staffed as if it were a stand-alone prison. There would be some savings or cost-efficiencies (or just better value for the same money). Common services may be able to be provided to some extent – food, laundry, site and infrastructure maintenance, and so on.'

[15] Some 'facts' are really values.

References

Arnold, H., Liebling, A. and Tait, S. (2007) 'Prison officers and prison culture', in Y. Jewkes (ed) *The prisons handbook*, Cullompton: Willan Publishing.
Bauman, Z. (1992) *Modernity and the Holocaust*, Cambridge: Polity Press.

Bottomley, A.K., Liebling, A. and Sparks, R. (1994) *An evaluation of Barlinnie and Shotts units*, Scottish Prison Service Occasional Papers no 7.

Boutellier, H. (2001) *Crime and morality: The significance of criminal justice in post-modern culture*, Dordrecht, Boston and London: Kluwer Academic Publishers.

Carter, P. (2003) *Managing offenders, reducing crime: A new approach*, London: Ministry of Justice.

Carter, P. (2007) *Securing the future: Proposals for the efficient and sustainable use of custody in England and Wales*, London: Ministry of Justice.

Christie, N. (1993) *Crime control as industry: Towards gulags, western style?* London: Routledge.

Corston, Baroness J. (2007) *The Corston Report: A review of women with particular vulnerabilities in the criminal justice system*, Home Office, London.

Crewe, B. (2008, forthcoming) *CAT-C: Power, adaptation and the social world of an English prison*, Oxford: Clarendon Press.

Daems, T. (2009, forthcoming) *Making sense of penal change: Punishment, victimization & society*, Oxford: Oxford University Press.

Downes, D. (1988) *Contrasts in tolerance: Post-war penal policy in the Netherlands and England and Wales*, Oxford: Oxford University Press.

Drake, D.H. (2007) 'A comparison of quality of life, legitimacy, and order in two maximum-security prisons', Cambridge University: unpublished PhD thesis.

Dryzek, J. (1995) 'Critical theory as a research program', in S.K. White (ed) *The Cambridge companion to Habermas*, Cambridge: Cambridge University Press, pp 97–119.

Feeley, M. and Simon, J. (1992) 'The new penology: Notes on the emerging strategy of corrections and its implications', *Criminology*, vol 30, no 4, pp 449–74.

Feeley, M. and Simon, J. (1994) 'Actuarial justice: The emerging new criminal law', in D. Nelken (ed) *The futures of criminology*, Sage, London, pp 173–201.

Gadd, V. and Shefer, G., with the assistance of Liebling, A., Tait, S. and McLean, C. (2006) 'Measuring the quality of prison life: Staff survey (pilot study)', unpublished report, Institute of Criminology, Cambridge University.

Garland, D. (1990) *Punishment and modern society*, Oxford: Clarendon Press.

Giddens, A. (1990) *Consequences of modernity*, Stanford, CA: Stanford University Press.

Giddens, A. (1998) *The third way: The renewal of social democracy*, Cambridge: Polity Press.

Hammerlin, Y. and Mathiassen, C. (2006) *Before and now: The consequences of changes in the interaction between prisoners and prison officers in some prisons*, Oslo: The Correctional Service Staff Academy, Reports 5/2006 (in Norweigian).

Home Office (1991) *Prison disturbances April 1990. Report of an Inquiry by the Rt Hon. Lord Justice Woolf (Parts I & II) and his Hon. Judge Stephen Tumin (Part III)*, London: Home Office.

Home Office (2001) *Modernising the management of the prison service: An independent report by the Targeted Performance Initiative Working Group – The Laming Report*, Home Office, London.

Jacobs, J.B. and Olitsky, E. (2004) 'Leadership and correctional reform', *PACE Law Review*, vol 24, no 2, pp 477–96.

Johnsen, B., Granheim, P-K. and Helgesen, J. (2008) 'The quality of working life for prison officers in high security prisons', paper presented at the International Conference on Prison Officers and Prison Culture, Orebro University, Sweden, April 2008, forthcoming as *The quality of prison life – a staff perspective: Does prison size matter?*

King, R.D. and McDermott, K. (1995) *The state of our prisons*, Oxford: Oxford University Press.

Liebling, A (1999) 'Prison suicide and prisoner coping', in M. Tonry and J. Petersilia (eds) *Prisons, crime and justice: An annual review of research*, vol 26, pp 283–360.

Liebling, A. assisted by Arnold, H. (2004) *Prisons and their moral performance: A study of values, quality and prison life*, Oxford: Clarendon Press.

Liebling, A. and Crewe, B. (in progress) 'Values, practices and outcomes in public and private sector corrections', Economic and Social Research Council Research Project.

Liebling, A. and Price, D. (2001) *The prison officer*, Leyhill: Prison Service (and Waterside Press).

Liebling, A., Durie, L., Stiles, A. and Tait, S. (2005) 'Revisiting prison suicide: The role of fairness and distress', in A. Liebling and S. Maruna (eds) *The effects of imprisonment*, Cullompton: Willan Publishing, pp 209–31.

Loader, I. (1998) 'Criminology and the public sphere: Arguments for utopian realism', in P. Walton and J. Young (eds) *The new criminology revisited*, London: Macmillan, pp 190–212.

Ministry of Justice (2008) *Titan prisons: Consultation paper CP10/08*, London: Ministry of Justice.

Prison Service (2007) *Background brief: Titan prisons*, London: HMSO.

Pusey, M. (1992) *Economic rationalism in Canberra: A nation-building state changes its mind*, Cambridge: Cambridge University Press.

Rock, P. (1995) 'The opening stages of criminal justice policy-making', *British Journal of Criminology*, vol 35, no 1, pp 1–16.

Sacks, J. (2000) *The politics of hope*, New York: Vintage Press.

Sennett, R. (2006) *The culture of the new capitalism (Castle lectures in ethics, politics & economics)*, New Haven, CT: Yale University Press.

Sparks, R. (1994) 'Can prisons be legitimate?' in R. King and M. McGuire (eds) *Prisons in context*, Oxford: Clarendon Press.

Sztompka, P. () *Trust: A sociological theory*, Cambridge: Cambridge University Press.

Tait, S. (2008) 'Prison officer care for prisoners in one men's and one women's prison', unpublished PhD thesis, Cambridge University.

Private punishment? An examination of the expansion, development and employment relations of private prisons

6

Sanjiv Sachdev

Introduction

The growth of private prisons is an important, controversial but relatively neglected issue in the broader debate around private sector involvement in public services. Despite the presence of private prisons in the UK since 1992, the existence of 11 private prisons with more in prospect and the centrality of labour management to the success of private prisons, there is limited consideration of its implications especially in relation to Prison Service workers. As the study of private prisons by James et al (1997, p viii) notes, employment relations matters have 'not been given the attention ... which it undoubtedly merits'. This echoes concerns in the US on the 'relatively scant body of research and evaluation of private prisons' (Greene, 2003, p 57; Camp and Gaes, 2001). According to Gaes et al (US) private prisons are an area characterised by 'more rhetoric than reality, more speculation than specifics and more postulation than proof' (2004, p xi). Similar issues arise in the UK; indeed the paucity of evidence behind significant policy shifts is a theme that recurs in the US (Gaes et al, 2004), the UK (Ryan and Ward, 1989; Ryan, 2003) and Australia (Moyle, 1993). For a government committed to evidence-based policy making this neglect is of concern.

However, a range of, mainly official, research on the impact of private prisons enables a relatively robust composite picture to be drawn. This includes work from the House of Commons Public Accounts Select Committee (House of Commons PAC), the Prison Service, the Prison Service Pay Review Body (PSPRB), the National Audit Office (NAO) and the Prison Inspectorate. The Confederation of British Industry (CBI), the Institute of Public Policy Research (IPPR) and the Prison Reform Trust (PRT)have also made significant contributions. This research is particularly important as the Prison Service has been promoted as a model for sectors such as health and education. A growing body of international evidence on the impact of the private sector provision of prison services is also emerging and can provide useful insights into the UK experience (for example, Logan, 1990; Moyle, 1993; PRT, 1994; Schior 1995; Harding, 1997; Camp and Gaes, 2001; Miller, 2003; Parenti, 2003; Gaes et al, 2004).

This paper outlines the rationale for the adoption of private prisons and identifies the ostensible attractions of such prisons as well as examining the centrality of competition. The key role of labour management and costs in private prisons are set out, the role of trade unions is considered, prior to a detailed evaluation of evidence in the Prison Service evidence. The employment relations implications of these developments are then examined. It follows Logan (1990, p 13) in using the term private prisons to cover those that are privately owned, operated or managed under contract to government. 'Prison Service' refers to the Prison Service of England and Wales.

The (re)embrace of the private sector

Both Conservative and Labour British governments have undergone sharp shifts in policy towards using the private sector in the criminal justice system; the case for private prisons (Adam Smith Institute, 1984; Logan, 1987; CBI, 2002) is now accepted by both. The Conservative Party, drawing on the experience of private prisons in the US, instigated the use of private prisons (Ryan and Ward, 1989; James et al 1997; Ryan 2003). Michael Howard MP, while Home Secretary, sought 'to create a [prison] private sector able to provide sustained competition … a genuinely mixed economy' (cited in McDonald, 1994, p 35). The policy shift was, in ideological terms, even more marked in the Labour Party. Until the mid-1990s the Labour Party had adamantly opposed prison privatisation: 'Labour will take back private prisons into public ownership – it is the only safe way forward' (John Prescott MP, 1994 cited in Nathan, 2003, p 168). In 1995, the then shadow Home Secretary, Jack Straw, declared that:

> The privatisation of the prison service is morally repugnant … It must be the direct responsibility of the state to look after those the courts decide it is in society's interests to imprison. It is not appropriate for people to profit out of incarceration. (cited in Harding, 1997)

In office there was a rapid volte-face; the Prison Service was extolled as a role model for private sector involvement and Private Finance Initiative became the dominant model of procurement for private prisons (IPPR, 2001; CBI, 2008).

The influence of the New Public Management (NPM) can be discerned in both major political parties. NPM maintains that government had become 'bloated, wasteful, ineffective' (Osborne and Gaebler, 1992, p 12), failing to change in a rapidly changing world. The NPM advocacy of greater private sector involvement in delivering public services is evident in the work of the Third Way thinker, Anthony Giddens, (2002, p 56) for whom 'Some of the inadequacies of Britain's public services are more to do with inertia, poor management, overmanning and bureaucratic sloth than lack of resources'. Similarly, a leading advocate of public/private partnerships (PPPs) and former Downing Street adviser, Julian Le Grand, maintains that in the 21st century 'Central government or local authorities will still be financing welfare services. But they will no longer be providing the service concerned or, if they do, their role will be increasingly that of a residual provider' (cited in Pike, 1996). A 'commitment to state withdrawal as direct service provider in favour of a more regulatory role through accounting audit and other instruments' is evident (Power, 1997, p 52). A consequence of this approach is the eradication of the limits of private sector involvement in the public services (Kelly, 2000).

Within a new framework of a remodelled, entrepreneurial government, competition has a primary role. The key distinction, argue proponents of NPM, is not public versus private, but monopoly versus competition, as the latter 'drives us to embrace innovation and strive for excellence' (Osborne and Gaebler, 1992, p 47). Moreover '[c]ompetition is the permanent force for innovation that government normally lacks' (p 92). The market and competition are paramount to reforming (better funded) public services. As the former prime minister stated: 'By instigating a competitive tendering process PPPs can also help to drive up cost efficiencies and encourage innovation in public service delivery' (Blair, 2002, p 14). In doing so he echoes Michael Howard MP, who as Home Secretary, announcing plans to extend private sector involvement in the Prison Service (1993) stated that 'There are encouraging signs that competition is a spur to higher standards and greater efficiency' (cited in PRT, 1996). An emergent political consensus in prison provision places faith in 'the innovative methods of the private sector' (Adam Smith Institute, 1984, p 64; see Sherwood, 2005, for Conservative Party policy) which is seen as a more efficient and effective provider of public services, with competition as the spur to these efficiencies (Davies and Freedland, 2007).

The Prison Service 'model'

The Prison Service has experienced a rapidly rising prison population without a corresponding increase in staff numbers. In 1993 the average prison population was 44,566; more recently it peaked at 82,068 (February 2008). This is expected to rise further, with official estimates predicting a population of 102,000 by 2014 (De Silva et al, 2007). At December 2007 it employed 51,129 staff (England and Wales), of whom 73% were prison officers (PSPRB, 2008, p xv); the staff/prisoner ratio has grown from 1.05 in 1993 to 1.5 in 2000 (Corby, 2002).

The reemergence of the private imprisonment industry has been a striking feature in the UK, the US and Australia (McDonald, 1994) and is also evident in Canada (2003) and South Africa (2003). The Prison Service is one with the most extensive evidence of the impact of Private Finance Initiative (PFI) schemes upon employment relations as well as one where wholesale privatisation has been considered.[1] PFI has existed in the service for over a decade – private prisons hold around 7% of prisoners (NAO, 2003). The proportion of prisoners held in privately managed prisons in the UK is now greater than in the US (Carter, 2003), although lower than Australia's (Harding, 1997).

This sector is also important, as the CBI notes, because unlike other areas of public service reform, the role of the private sector goes 'beyond traditional facilities management and infrastructure support: it has taken on and delivered core public service goals' (CBI, 2003, p 7). In prison PFI projects the contractor provides the whole service, including custody, education and healthcare for prisoners, whereas in projects such as new hospitals and schools the public sector remains responsible for the provision of staff such as nurses and teachers. The IPPR (2001), citing the experience of the Prison Service, concluded that the separations in health and education should be removed.

Both the former Prime Minister and the then Chancellor cited the Prison Service as a model PFI success. According to the then Prime Minister, the private sector has precipitated 'major improvements in the way that public prisons are operated with considerable efficiency gains' (Blair, 2002, p 16). The former Chancellor cited the management of prisons as one of the 'areas [where] we can show that the use of private contractors is not at the expense of the public interest or need be at the expense of terms and conditions of employees but, if we can secure greater efficiency in the provision of the service, it is one means by which the public interest is advanced' (Brown, 2003). As argued below, these claims are highly questionable.

Competition, contestability and future prospects

In accordance with the precepts of New Public Management, competition is viewed as a means of instigating change. For Phillipa Drew – the then operational director of the Prison Service – the point of market testing 'was not actually to do it, but to use the continuing threat of it to stimulate better performance'. While this approach attracted the opprobrium of the then Home Secretary, subsequent events seem to have borne out this approach – it seems to be the essence of recent policy (Lewis 1997, p 180). Explaining the rationale for confining some bids to the private sector, Derek Lewis stated that:

> For competition to be effective, there had to be a private sector large enough to ensure a continued commitment of money and management by the firms involved. We decided that a minimum of twelve establishments, or 10 per cent of the total number of prisons, were needed under private management to create the necessary critical mass. (Lewis, 1997, p 89)

Market testing does appear to have had some effect on the working practices of public sector prisons. At HMP Woodhill, then a new public sector prison, '[t]here was considerable recognition that the threat of market-testing had concentrated the minds of all those who had responsibility for financial matters to reduce unit costs and improve overall efficiency ... and the traditional resistance to change and adherence to custom was unable to survive in this climate' (James et al, 1997, p 127). More generally, contracting out and market testing was 'a highly significant factor in public sector prisons and was consciously used by senior management at Woodhill as part of their efforts to change working practices and staff attitudes' (p 172). However, as James et al also note, 'to attribute the many achievements of Woodhill solely to [market testing] would be to tell only part of the story' (p 172).

Further expansion of private sector provision is in prospect with plans to install a quasi-market to foster competition as a 'stimulus' for change, contain costs, nurture innovation and provide a benchmark against which to measure public sector prisons.

The Carter Report saw 'a danger that the full benefits of contestability will not be realised if the involvement of the private sector is limited to new and failing prisons. Private providers need to be given an incentive to invest if they are to continue to be a credible alternative to public sector providers' (Carter, 2003, p 24) and argued for a programme of market testing to attract new providers from private and voluntary sectors into the market (p 34). The report's proposal of the public sector provider as an operating arm of the National Offender Management Service (NOMS) acting on a level playing field with other private operators (p 36) was accepted by the Home Office. The Home Office regards the experience of using the private sector as being 'extremely positive' (Home Office, 2004, p 10) and seeks to encourage 'the greater use of the private and "not-for-profit" sectors in prisons ... wherever it can demonstrate greater cost effectiveness' (Home Office, 2004, para 27). Central to the Carter Report and Home Office proposals is 'contestability', with places to be commissioned from the provider, either public or private, offering the most effective services at best value. As the market develops, it is envisaged that offender managers will be able to buy custodial places from any sector, public or private 'based only on their cost effectiveness in reducing re-offending' (Home Office, 2004, p 10). Public sector prisons are expected to compete on the basis of cost with the private sector:

> For public sector prisons to deliver cost effective performance in the future, it is imperative that they are competitive with the best in the private sector. (David Blunkett, Home Secretary 2004; see PSPRB, 2005, p 47)

In August 2006, a NOMS paper published further plans in *Improving prison and probation services: Public value partnership*. These reforms offer the potential for significant growth in private sector provision. Carter is reported to envisage about 20% of prisons being managed by the private sector (DLA MCG, 2004, p 18). Intriguingly, in 1996 representatives of the private prison firms had said that they would like to see between 20 and 25% of the prison estate shared among three to five companies (cited in Nathan, 2003, p 175) – in September 2006 the 11 private prisons were managed by four different companies (DLA MCG, 2006).

Concerns have developed on the practical effects of the competitive process. Liebling found that '[t]he competitive process generally results in high quality ambitious bids which are, in practice, challenging to deliver ... Cost cutting and aspirations to "perform" can go too far in this climate, resulting in an overstretched workforce and high risks to the establishment's functioning' (Liebling, 2004, p 105). Competition has also, arguably, stifled collaboration. Ann Owers, the chief inspector of prisons, identified a reluctance to share good practice because one sector (public or private])did not want to give 'the competitive edge' to the other. Direct competition had, according to Owers, 'a tendency towards hoarding of good practice rather than sharing' (cited in Burns, 2005b).

The centrality of labour management and costs in private prisons

From their inception, changing labour practices were central to the success of the private prisons. As early as 1984 the Adam Smith Institute argued that private prisons would use 'manpower more effectively' (Adam Smith Institute, 1984, p 66) than the public sector. Contractors said they were able to run prisons more 'efficiently' through their use of labour; 'by reduc[ing] staff numbers by introducing more flexible working practices, and by a greater use of improved technology' (Deliotte, Haskins and Sells, 1989, cited in James et al, 1997, p 54). The IPPR Commission maintains that 'it is precisely in the area of the organisation of work that the private sector might make a significant contribution to the management of public services' (IPPR, 2001, p 201). This is unsurprising given the highly labour intensive nature of many public services; in the Prison Service, staff costs account for about 80% of prison running costs (NAO, 2003, p 33).

The 2001 IPPR Commission report – mostly a comprehensive study of the issues arising from PPPs – devotes just nine and a half of its 246 pages to examining workforce issues, compared, for example, to some 34 pages on the – important – issue of accountability. Workforce issues do not even merit a chapter of their own. The Carter Report asserts that 'the introduction of performance testing has been successful in driving down costs, changing the culture and enabling flexible staffing structures to be introduced' on the sole (and slender) basis of a CBI report (Carter, 2003, p 24).

A more recent IPPR report (Maltby and Gosling, 2003) confines itself to the issue of the two-tier workforce. This too neglects much of the literature in this area and seemingly adopts employer assumptions of 'rigid public sector working practices' (p 3) or 'restrictive practices' (p 9) impeding employers' ability to organise their workforces. However, it does explicitly articulate the key governmental concern behind its reluctance to regulate this area, namely the belief that there is 'a fundamental trade off: flexibility of staff deployment versus protection of staff terms and conditions'. Staff in PFI prisons are younger (about 12% were under 25, compared with about 3% in the public sector), more likely to be women (34% compared with 21%) and tend to have 'little or no prior experience of working in prisons' (NAO, 2003, p

25). However, it is hard to see why, as the IPPR contend (Maltby and Gosling, 2003, p 5), 'employing relatively more women, younger staff and staff who do not have a history of working in the prison service' justifies the lower terms and conditions or renders such comparisons 'not directly comparable'. Indeed the PSPRB shows such comparisons to be both eminently possible and credible, finding that 'Private sector prison roles up to senior officer level were broadly equivalent to, or at some prisons slightly greater than, Prison service roles' (PSPRB, 2003, p 18). For the key prison officer/prison custody officer grade the assessment of the consultants hired by the PSPRB was that it was generally 'a closely equivalent role' (DLA MCG, 2003, p 38). In the event of disturbances or other serious incidents prison staff from neighbouring prisons have assisted each other.[2] Consequently, there have been public and private sector prison staff working alongside one another, doing the same work, for markedly different rates of pay.

Taming of the unions: the disciplining of labour

A related issue to labour management is trade union containment. The industrial relations climate in British prisons in the 1970s and 1980s has been characterised as one of 'acrimony and distrust' (Rutherford, 1990, p 60). The former Director-General described the Prison Officers Association (POA) as 'the principal obstacle to progress' (Lewis, 1997, p 137), characterising it as 'a union caught in a 1960s timewarp, enforcing unnecessary overtime, protecting excessive manning levels and successfully undermining or usurping management decisions' (p 131). His successor, Sir Richard Tilt, described industrial relations as being 'difficult' (House of Commons PAC, 1999). The POA was seen as 'very important in placing constraints on modernization' (Liebling, 2004, p 402). The influential analysis of King and McDermott found that 'For many years the cost-effectiveness of the prison system has been a cause for concern, and there have been a number of attempts to gain a more efficient use of resources, especially manpower' (King and McDermott, 1989, p 126). James et al (1997, p 47) contended that the members of the POA 'exercised a substantial amount of control over the nature and delivery of prison regimes and whose practices led to increasing staff levels and high levels of overtime'.

Concern at the power of the POA chimed with the broader Thatcherite assault on trade unions. The desire to break the influence of the POA was key to the promotion of the private sector in the Prison Service. The Adam Smith Institute complained of 'producer dominance' (Young, 1987, p 4). In the early 1990s the *Times* argued that privatisation should be used to combat the industrial muscle of the POA whose capacity to block prison reform 'rested on its membership monopoly provider' offering their services to a single buyer, the government (cited in Ryan, 2003, p 102).

Replicating the rationale of private sector involvement in local government (Sachdev, 2001, p 23) and health (Willets, 1993), privatisation was seen as a means of reducing union power. For some privatisation was 'a stick with which to beat the POA' (cited in Ryan, 1994, p 2) – a mechanism to 'tame' it, as 'contracting threatens their [union members'] jobs and, more significantly, their power' (Logan, 1990, p 11). It is argued that the 'pressure to compete forces a reconsideration and change of work rules that have been built up in the public sector. Inefficient practices will be more difficult to support if one's employment is at risk.' (McDonald, 1994, p 38). The concept of 'inefficiency' used here needs closer attention, but there is little doubt that the Prison Service uses employees' fear of losing their livelihoods to instigate changes in labour practices, thus the Home Office (2004, p 10) notes that Dartmoor and Liverpool Prisons transformed their performance in response to '*the threat* of the private sector' (author's italics). As a consequence of privatisation 'the workforce would be more controlled, less unionised and less secure' (James et al, 1997, p 8). Lewis criticised the then Home Secretary Michael Howard's 'apparent belief that fear is the principal tool of motivation', but this would seem to ignore that this is the essence of the effect of competition in the Prison Service (Lewis 1997, p 119).

The Prison Service describes its relationship with the Prison Service trade unions as 'positive' (HM Prison Service, 2003, p 39). The Prison Officers Association is the main recognised Prison Service union, with 31,845 members in 2000 in England and Wales (cited in Corby, 2002).[3] In none of the 11 private prisons has the POA gained recognition for collective bargaining purposes despite a number of applications to the Central Arbitration Committee (Bach, 2002). The private sector prison provider Global Solutions Limited recognises GMB, the trade union, for bargaining purposes at its prisons (CBI, 2003). There is a small breakaway union, the Prison Services Union, which has 4,103 members, but is not recognised by the Prison Service, although the Serco Institute (Serco being a leading private prison firm) and UK Detention Services do so.

The POA itself seems to have seriously underestimated the staying power of private prisons. The assistant secretary of the POA argued in 1987 that the weight of argument against private prisons would mean that it would be 'nothing more than a distasteful experiment' (cited in Rutherford, 1990, p 60) – indeed initially it did not recruit members in the private sector (and thus, arguably opened up scope for GMB, which did so).

Employment relations in the Prison Service: an evaluation

Unlike other public services, there is substantial evidence of the impact of privately managed prisons on pay and conditions and other labour issues (DLA MCG, 2006; Sachdev, 2004; DLA MCG, 2004; PSPRB, 2005). There is little contention that UK private prisons are generally cheaper (but not always) to run than public sector ones; the Home Office found that, on average, private prisons cost 2% more to 11% less than comparable state prisons (Andrewes, 2000).[4] However, the source of these lower costs is more debatable. The evidence that does exist is considered under the separate headings of pay and conditions, labour turnover, pensions and other benefits, staffing levels and staff performance.

Pay and conditions: claims and reality

Advocates of prison privatisation have argued that private prisons, as well as leading to 'dramatic improvements in conditions for prisoners', did 'not adversely affect public sector prison employees' who are offered jobs 'at similar or increased levels of pay' (Young 1987, p 38). Indeed, some US firms were said to offer 'better working conditions and higher pay' (p 35). Similarly the Kennedy Report in Australia argued that privatisation would bring 'an important element of competition for Correctional Officers which would ultimately lift their status, pay and conditions' (1988, p 93, cited in Moyle, 1993). In the UK the then Prime Minister said that PFI projects will lead to 'better terms and conditions' (Blair, 2002); the Treasury claimed that PFI is only used 'where the value for money it offers is not at the cost of terms and conditions of staff' (HM Treasury, 2003). More recently, the Serco Institute claimed that 'basic pay rates' in the UK and US are 'often comparable' (Sturgess and Smith, 2006a, p 10 and 2006b, p 77).

However, the evidence corroborates the (1998) conclusion of the House of Commons Public Accounts Committee that the cheaper running costs of private sector prisons 'was almost wholly to do with different wage rates and different staff levels, and also pension arrangements, sick leave arrangements and different lengths of the working week' and a Home Office study finding that the 'difference in staff costs accounts for all the difference between the sectors' (Andrewes, 2000, p 4).

The evidence that the pay and conditions in private prisons are markedly inferior to those in the public sector is overwhelming and mostly uncontested. Table 6.1, from research commissioned by the PSPRB, clearly illustrates the sharp difference in pay and conditions (DLA MCG, 2006).

For prison officers, the private sector pay packages are significantly inferior to those in the public sector. Average basic pay is sharply lower (public sector rates are some 39% higher); when the value of pension and holiday benefits are added this difference rises to 61%. The overall pay scales are much more modest, the contracted working hours longer, the overtime and annual leave arrangements less favourable (public sector staff get, on average, 7.5 days more leave) and, crucially, pension provision is markedly inferior. Importantly, as private sector rates are comparators in the PSPRB analysis for the public sector, they now act as a potential drag on most public sector rates.

The inferiority of private sector pensions is particularly evident (the Serco Institute concedes that 'fringe benefits', such as pensions, are 'less generous'; Sturgess and Smith 2006a, p 10; 2006b, p 77). The contributions for Prison Service staff give them

Table 6.1: Comparison of pay and conditions for prison officers and prison custody officers (2006)

	Prison officer (public)	Prison custody officer (private)
Average starting basic pay	£17,744	£16,005 (39 hr week)
Average basic pay	£23,926	£17,435
Pay range	£17,744–£26,858	On average £4,000
Average weekly contracted hrs	39	39–42
Overtime pay	Time off in lieu, or up to 9 hrs a week at standard rate	None, flat rate or 1.5x
Pension	Final salary scheme (retirement at 60). Employer contribution equivalent to 21.5%	Money purchase scheme (retirement at 65). Employer contribution 6.2%; employee contribution 3.6%
Annual leave (days)	25–33 (7.5 days more on average)	20–23

Source: DLA MCG Consulting (2006)

guaranteed benefits, whereas those for most private sector staff do not; moreover, the Prison Service retirement age is 60 whereas it is 65 for many company staff. While there has been a trend in the private sector to shift investment risk from the company to the individual, public sector pensions have been 'comfortably above the amounts that have been going into all but the very best private sector final salary schemes' (Timmins, 2002). This pattern is replicated in the patterns of public and private Prison Service provision. The effect of the government's policy has been to relegate private prison workers, at the very time it expresses general concern at the insufficiency of work-based pension provision, from a relatively generous pension scheme to a much inferior one.

The CBI ascribes the difference in pay primarily to private prisons 'pay rates reflect[ing] local economic conditions' whereas Prison Service pay is set by 'national wage bargaining'[5] and thus 'influenced to some extent by the cost of living in the most expensive parts of the UK' (CBI, 2003, p 40). However, research undertaken by the PSPRB found that these markedly lower pay levels could not be wholly ascribed to private prisons being in areas of high unemployment:

> About half the privately-managed prisons and all of the immigration centres are in areas where unemployment is at or below the national average, including several that are operating in highly competitive local labour markets. Pay rates in these

cases are still well below public sector levels. This suggests that the key drivers for pay levels in the private companies are not only local labour markets but also commercial pressures imposed by the contracts they have entered into to manage various custodial services. (PSPRB, 2003, p 19)

Moreover, contrary to claims made by the CBI, rather than narrowing differentials between the private and public sectors, regional locality payments accorded to prison officers (varying between £1,400 and £4,000 a year) mean that in the South East 'the lead of Prison Officers over their private sector counterparts is likely to be greater than elsewhere' (DLA MCG 2004, p 29).

Tentative evidence from case studies finds staff morale to be a problem. In the Wolds prison 73% of main grade and middle management staff interviewed felt that staff morale was poor to moderate (cited in James et al, 1997). Indeed, 'from the staff perspective, the achievements of Wolds and other private sector prisons may be at the cost of higher levels of stress and greater job insecurity for many of those recruited to work in them'(p 137).

The CBI concedes that private prisons pay their prison officers 'significantly less than the Prison Service' (CBI, 2003, p 39). Richard Tilt, the former Director-General of the Prison Service in England and Wales, told the House of Commons PAC that (private sector prison) 'pay rates are lower, pension provision is generally poorer in the private sector and all those contribute to bring the cost down' (House of Commons PAC, 1999, para 210). Moreover, before the introduction of competition, 'it was very difficult to negotiate *down* pay rates and conditions of service ... it becomes a slightly more viable option once you get a degree of competition' (House of Commons PAC, 1999, para 232, emphasis added). Competition is not seen as a force for higher pay.

Intriguingly, the CBI state that some of the prison management companies may have 'engaged in aggressive competition to build market share' and faltered since, intimating that companies were running early contracts as loss leaders to get a foothold in a burgeoning market. Moreover, it contends that the government needs to recognise

the wider implications of procurement processes that use price as the dominant criterion in evaluating successful bids. With core public services such as prison management, government must always be concerned with procuring social outcomes. This may extend to defining acceptable minima for the terms and conditions of staff members as well as ensuring the welfare and security of prisoners. (CBI, 2003, p 42)

Consideration of such 'wider implications' remains elusive.

Some striking parallels are to be found with US private prisons. The entry-level salary paid by private prisons to guards (2000) is $17,628 compared with $23,002 in the public sector; the average maximum salary differential is greater still – $22,082 to

$36,328 (cited in Greene, 2003, p 63). According to Camp and Gaes (2001, p 2): 'The extent that private prisons can be operated more cheaply than their public sector counterparts ... the savings will most likely come from lower wages/or benefits, fewer staff, or both.' The inexperience of staff and understaffing has been a recurrent criticism of US private prisons (Greene, 2003).

Labour turnover in prisons

Private prison advocates, mainly in the US, have argued that one outcome of private prisons would be lower labour turnover rates. Thus Moore (1999, p 215) argues that 'A commonly used method of measuring job satisfaction of private sector workers ... is to examine the 'quit rate' or labor turnover rate. If workers are leaving the firm or industry more rapidly than normal, then this typically means that wages or benefits are too low, or job conditions are unsatisfactory.' Logan contends that 'there is no substitute for experience, which accumulates over time in an efficient stable work force' (Logan, 1990, p 132) and rates of turnover are useful 'to comparatively evaluate governmental and private prisons'. Moreover, 'turnover is at least easy to measure and it is one of several factors that can be used to evaluate prison quality' (p 133). For Young, low turnover is a reflection of higher morale (Young, 1987, p 15) and improved conditions (p 35).

In practice, labour turnover rates have been much higher in the private sector. High levels of labour turnover are a serious problem and cost in many UK private prisons. Overall, among prison custody officers the resignation rate is 24% – nearly 10 times greater than the 3% rate among public sector prison officers (DLA MCG, 2006). In 2003, this figure masked regional differences; while in private prison establishments in the North rates averaged 13%, in the Midlands and South this rose to 32% (one had a rate of 49%). High levels of turnover 'caused continuing problems in maintaining staff levels. This put more pressure on existing staff and further exacerbated turnover difficulties' (PSPRB, 2004, p 19). According to the National Audit Office, there was 'a very high turnover of staff in most private prisons and in each case the turnover was higher than the public sector' (NAO, 2003, p 26). The Serco Institute ascribes 'maintaining a higher turnover rate' (Sturgess and Smith, 2006a, p 10; 2006b, p 77) as one of the reasons why private prisons have 'less costly terms of employment'.

The lower salaries of private sector staff when compared with their public sector equivalents was, according to the NAO, 'likely to be a factor in the high levels of turnover, particularly in areas of relatively low unemployment' (NAO, 2003, p 26). The level of the pay and benefits package and the 'absence of much opportunity for pay progression' (PSPRB, 2004, p 19) contributed to the 'continuing high turnover' in some private prisons. In 2003 the PSPRB reported that three of the seven PFI prisons[6] 'appear unable to offer salaries which are sufficiently attractive to meet the staffing levels stipulated in their contract bids. This can have serious consequences for staffing levels, the quality of staffing employed and their retention levels' (PSPRB,

2003, p 32).[7] One factor in the high turnover in private prisons is competition from better paid jobs in the public sector Prison Service (as well as the police and probation services). The Prison Service is, however, concerned that turnover is too low in the public sector as 'it is difficult to move forward and change things' (Phil Wheatley, Director-General of the Prison Service in House of Commons PAC, 2003), although it has difficulties recruiting in areas with particularly buoyant local labour markets (PSPRB, 2004, p 15).

A similar pattern prevails in the US. The turnover rate for US private prisons reached 52% in 2000, compared with 16% for US public prisons (cited in Greene, 2003, p 63). According to Gaes et al, 'nearly half of all private prisons in the US experienced a turnover rate of at least 50 per cent in a six-month period between February and July 1999' (Gaes et al, 2004, p 113). This rate was 'much greater on average in the private sector' (p 114). Parenti (2003, p 36) cites one private prison in Florida with an annual staff turnover of 200%.

Labour turnover is not a dog that refuses to bark – there is a widespread recognition of the issue but, rather curiously, it is a bark that is not heeded. It is not an issue that has been subject to wider scrutiny or attention, for example by the Public Accounts Committee, in a similar way, for example, to that of sickness absence.

The impact of the private sector on prison service performance

PFI contractors have brought some innovations, although the overall picture is variable. The NAO (2003, p 7) found that 'the best PFI prisons are outperforming most public prisons but the lowest performing PFI prison is among the worst in the prison estate'. It was a PFI prison, Ashfield, that the Chief Prison Inspector described as 'probably the most depressing I have issued' (Owers in HM Chief Inspector of Prisons (HMCIP), 2002a, p 3).[8] In one Prison Inspectorate report, the Chief Inspector stated that the PFI prison concerned should 'be a salutary reminder that the Commissioner's commitment to expose failing public sector prisons to private sector competition ("performance testing") will not always deliver an immediate private sector panacea' (HMCIP, 2003a, p 5).

As to their use of staff, the House of Commons PAC concluded that 'Shift patterns in PFI prisons allow receptions to open later, visiting times to be more flexible and prisoners on enhanced regimes to eat with their families'. As a result of these innovations, staffing changes were introduced by the Prison Service in public sector prisons (House of Commons PAC, 2003, p 8). Paid sickness absence was also markedly lower – although recent figures found a sharp convergence in these rates, with the older workforce of the Prison Service having an absence rate of 13.3 days, compared with 12.5 for the private sector (which also had markedly less generous schemes (NAO, 2004)). There is 'little difference in terms of the daily routines of prisons' (NAO, 2003, p 7). Private prisons generally performed better on the Prison Service's decency agenda, such as respect shown to prisoners. However, 'they generally perform less well in areas such as safety and security' (NAO, 2003, p 24) – the NAO and House of Commons PAC concluding that the balance between the two areas appears to be difficult for any prison to achieve, whether private or public.

As a whole, this evidence concludes that while some innovation (the heading of a 'small amount of innovation' is used by the National Audit Office (2004, p 33)) from the private sector is evident, the overall picture is of a 'mixed' performance (NAO, 2004, p 6); this much more muted evaluation is at odds with the appraisal of the Carter Report or the claims of the CBI (2008).

James et al (1997, p 131) examined six new prisons and found 'there was evidence of similar or greater innovation by prison management in some of the public sector prisons'. They found innovation was far from being a monopoly of the private sector: 'There can be no doubt, therefore, that innovation in regime delivery plus high-quality, committed and effective senior management are to be found as much in new public sector prisons as in those where the management has been contracted-out to private companies.' (James et al, 1997, p 132).

The NAO also found that while there seemed to be greater 'operational flexibility' (more flexible visiting times, wider shift patterns), the private sector 'has been less successful in developing its staff for senior management roles. Directors at private prisons have been recruited from the ranks of experienced Prison Service governors rather than internally[9] (despite the fact that contractors have been managing prisons for 15 years). The private sector is therefore 'benefiting from the experience and skills of former employees' (NAO, 2003, p 33). The CBI contends that 'NOMS should do more to recruit high calibre managers from outside the existing offender mgt service' (CBI, 2008, p 22) but does not note that private prison governors do not bring in new expertise from the private sector but derive almost wholly by being poached from the public sector.

IPPR research notes that 'Detailed qualitative work needs to be undertaken to examine whether savings delivered by the private sector are secured at the expense of quality and equity' (Thompson, 2000, p 152). Home Office research also finds that when the cost per baseline place is measured against the cost per use in-place, little or no saving is produced; indeed when one prison was removed from calculations privately managed prisons 'were actually two to three per cent more expensive than their public sector comparators' (Park, 2000, p 24). This research found that private sector prisons were also more overcrowded.

Within Prison Service ranks there is also the view that while competition does have an effect in improving performance, it is a one-off effect – it is not sustained. As time passes, early advantages wear off and some of the disadvantages become more apparent. Martin Narey, the former director of Prison Services, argued that the private sector gave a 'massive step forward in the use of staff' but 'they have become, in running prisons, a bit complacent. They have not been as imaginative as this service has had to become in terms of utilising staff, and, of course, they have to take a profit out of this.' (cited in Brown, 2001).

Staffing levels

While pressures on staffing levels are ubiquitous across the private and public sector, it appears to be a more significant issue in the private sector. Thus 'the issue of staffing levels within the [private] prison was one that was a source of continuing concern for management and staff' (James et al, 1997, p 76) – 80% of the staff interviewed were dissatisfied with the staffing levels; 71% thought that there were not enough staff to run the prison safely, a perception shared by prisoners. As a result of inadequate staffing levels, many found themselves working 60 hours a week and 'staff found that they were continually being asked to come in on their rest days to cover staffing shortages' (James et al, 1997, p 78). Staff also saw this issue as related to Group 4's profit levels. A later study 'witnessed directors of privately managed prisons reluctantly following the instructions of their company directors to reduce staffing levels, and make additional savings' (Liebling, 2004, p 120; this tension was also evident in public prisons too).

The inexperience of PFI prison staff and low staffing levels are a recurring concern of the Prison Inspectorate (HMCIP, 2002a; 2002b; 2003a; 2003b). The low staffing levels are in part a consequence of a 'downward pressure on the price of recent contracts' (House of Commons PAC, 2003, p 9). The Home Office also had concerns about staffing levels at two of the public prisons – Manchester and Blakenhurst – operating under Service Level Agreements and won by tender from the private sector.[10] It thus appears that while in-house bids have been successful in winning prison contracts, this seems to be at the cost of staff numbers.

However, as a mechanism of cost containment, private prisons appear to have been more successful. Indeed the 'most decisive practical consideration influencing the appeal of private sector prisons was cost' (James et al, 1997, p 8); according to Richard Tilt, private prisons were 'broadly successful within the objectives set for the policy of introducing competition as a way of moderating/controlling unit costs. It was much less successful in terms of encouraging innovation of which we did not see a great deal. Most providers were too nervous to take too many risks' (Tilt, 2005).

The impact on prison productivity

Efficiency is itself a contested concept (Wolff, 2004). Public service productivity is 'notoriously difficult to measure' (Balls et al, 2003, p 327). PFI prisons are praised for 'delivering higher productivity' (Andrewes, 2000, p 10; CBI, 2003). However, the problems with measuring public service productivity are well known[11] (Power,

1997; O'Neil, 2002). Measurable indices are known to often take precedence over meaningful ones, thus '[p]rivate sector contracts have tended to focus on the quantity, rather than quality, of provision and this needs to be addressed' (Owers in HMCIP, 2003b, p 4). Moreover, as Liebling notes (2004, p 68), 'Targets tend to be set in areas that are amenable to measurement, rather than in areas that 'matter' … Wormwood Scrubs has been used as an example of a prison that was 'failing' and yet apparently effective according to its KPI performance.'

Overall, there were 17% fewer staff per prisoner in private prisons. Working hours in privately managed prisons were 3% longer and planned time off (including holidays and bank holidays) was on average 13% lower. While paid sickness absence was often markedly lower, the NAO (2004), as noted above, found a sharp convergence in sickness rates. This meant that private sector employees spent 7% more time at work than public sector ones, which in turn is 'one of the reasons why contracted prisons can operate with fewer staff' (Andrewes, 1998). The most important part of this difference was due to the longer hours worked by contracted prison staff, followed closely by lower sickness absence levels (Andrewes, 2000). Thus, while some of this higher 'productivity' arises from better sickness management, much more is a consequence of longer hours – which made 'the greatest difference' to productivity (CBI, 2003, p 39) – and shorter holidays. 'Productivity improvements' are thus primarily an increase in workloads through longer hours (at lower pay rates) and shorter holidays, that is, at the expense of terms and conditions. Interestingly, in its account of productivity in prisons the Serco Institute made no mention of longer hours and less leave (Sturgess and Smith, 2006a, 2006b).

Conclusion

Despite some 15 years of controversy, the scale and importance of the initiative and the large numbers of employees affected by it, the implications of private prisons have been seriously neglected. The evidence that does exist suggests serious grounds for concern, with private prisons fostering a significant deterioration in the terms and conditions, particularly among relatively low-paid staff. Future problems may have been set in store by the poor pension provision of many private providers of public services, both in terms of greater pensioner poverty and increased demands upon the state. Attention to the workforce issue has been both belated and limited. Insufficient attention has been paid to the mounting evidence of official agencies that much, if not most, of the cost advantage of private contractors is at the expense of terms and conditions rather than from innovation. Although some evidence of Prison Service innovation exists, it is not on the scale warranted by the rhetoric around the virtues of PFI/competition. Nor is there any evidence as to why innovation should entail a degradation of employee pay and conditions.

The Treasury maintains that PFI is only used 'where the value for money it offers is not at the cost of the terms and conditions of staff' (HM Treasury, 2003, p 2).

This seems at odds with the evidence in the Prison Service from the Pay Review Body, House of Commons Public Accounts Committee, the National Audit Office, the Prison Service and the CBI. Indeed, such are trends in this area that a former Secretary of State called for steps 'to halt the development of a two tier workforce in which private sector employees suffer worse pay and conditions' (Byers, 2003).

Confusion seems apparent as to the effect of competition upon pay and conditions; the former Prime Minister suggests that it leads to 'better pay and conditions' (Blair, 2002, p 26); the Treasury writes of 'protecting' pay and pensions (HM Treasury, 2003, p 69), while the former head of the Prison Service speaks of the difficulty in negotiating 'down pay rates and conditions of service' (House of Commons PAC, 1999).

Competition can and has exerted a downward pressure upon pay and conditions in what are highly labour-intensive services. The Prison Service experience suggests that many 'efficiency gains' are secured by three key means: reducing staff numbers and gradings; lowering the average individual remuneration; and work intensification through longer working hours and shorter annual leave as well as better staff sickness management, that is, there is a wealth transfer rather than genuine innovation. Issues of lower staffing levels and high labour turnover rates are insufficiently addressed.

Furthermore, while New Labour has presided over a revival of public-service employment levels, there has been no corresponding renewal of a public-service ethic or a new settlement on labour standards. The absence of a coherent approach to public sector employment relations has led to 'an urgent need for a principled approach towards the regulation of public service employment' beyond the establishment of a Public Sector Employment Forum to share best practice (Morris, 2000, p 170). Public sector employment is distinctive in that 'the principle of democratic accountability implies a series of constraints on the State's autonomy as employer which are not imposed upon employers in the private sector' (Morris, 2000, p 174). These include requirements of transparency, information accountability, public scrutiny in the use of public money and 'equal access'-based recruitment, promotion, disciplinary and dismissal mechanisms.

This neglect and the delegation of 'innovation' to the private sector has allowed the degradation of terms and conditions in many public services. Moreover, the failure to embed a new consensus around fair employment standards for public-service workers generally renders such gains highly fragile and vulnerable to a change of government. This is particularly important amid the wider debate on securing 'savings' in public services.

A new Conservative government could find the Prison Service 'model' for pay and conditions an attractive one to be extended to health and education, with sharply reduced pay and conditions being a source of public spending 'savings', regardless of their impact on the workforce itself.

Notes

[1] It was only the reinterpretation of the Transfer of Undertakings (TUPE) regulations by the European Court of Justice that prevented the then Conservative Home Secretary, Kenneth Clarke, 'from privatising up to twenty existing prisons at a stroke. It is also, obviously, another reason why only the private sector is being allowed to bid for newly built prisons' (Ryan, 1994, p 3). According to a leaked letter from him: 'In relation to prison education services, my view is that the consequences [of the TUPE case] are very damaging because we stand to lose almost all the efficiency and cost savings achieved if all existing staff have to be taken on by new contractors on their present terms and conditions' (cited in Foley, 1994, p 24). According to Lewis (1997) Sir Peter Levene, the then Prime Minister's (John Major) efficiency adviser, believed that the whole service could be contracted out to the private sector.

[2] An incident at Lincoln prison and one involving Parc PFI prison is cited by the House of Commons PAC (2003).

[3] In Scotland the SPOA play a similar role.

[4] A narrowing of differences from the 1998 study is generally evident; the 'difference in staffing ratios narrowed significantly' (Andrewes, 2000, p 2).

[5] This is not wholly accurate as the review body system, of which the Prison Service has been part since 2001, is not a form of 'bargaining', but involves an independent standing body making representations to the government after considering submissions from interested parties. They have been introduced to replace collective bargaining (Fredman and Morris, 1990).

[6] Rye Hill, Dovegate and Ashfield.

[7] The poor quality of education at Ashfield seems due 'to the high turnover and quality of staff' – 10% of teaching staff were leaving per month.

[8] In May 2002 the Prison Service had taken over direct management from the contractor although this has since returned to the contractor.

[9] Indeed 'Directors' [pay] packages have been particularly geared to attracting Governors from the Prison Service' (DLA MCG, 2003, p 4).

[10] In the former the Prison Inspectorate expressed concerns that staff numbers, which had been reduced by 270 (30%), had been cut to 'unsafe' levels (HMCIP, 2001, p 4).

[11] The following from the House of Commons Treasury Select Committee (2004) is illustrative: 'We note the evidence given by Treasury officials to our Sub-committee in September last year that a target for 2.5% efficiency savings set in an earlier Spending

Review for the Treasury itself had been dropped in part because "it has not been possible to measure efficiency for the whole of the Treasury in quite those terms'".

References

Adam Smith Institute (1984) *Omega report, justice policy*, London: Adam Smith Institute.

Andrewes, C. (1998) Memorandum by HM Prison Service, 8 April, HM Prison Service, www.publications.parliament.uk/pa/cm199798/cmselect/cmpubacc/499/8012102. htm

Andrewes, C. (2000) *Contracted and publicly managed prisons: Cost and staffing comparisons 1997–98*, London: HM Prison Service.

Bach, S.D. (2002) 'Public sector employment relations under Labour: Muddling through on modernisation', *British Journal of Industrial Relations*, vol 40, no 2, June, pp 319–39.

Balls E., O'Donnell, G. and Grice, J. (2003) *Microeconomic reform in Britain: Delivering opportunities for all*, Basingstoke: Palgrave Macmillan.

Blair, T. (2002) *The courage of our convictions: Why reform of the public services is the route to social justice*, Fabian Ideas 603, London: Fabian Society.

Brown, G. (2003) 'A modern agenda for prosperity and social reform', Speech by the Chancellor of the Exchequer to the Social Market Foundation, 3 February, www. hm-treasury.gov.uk

Brown, K. (2001) 'The prison service finds the best of both worlds', *Financial Times*, 2 October, p 18.

Burns, J. (2005b) 'Government reviews private sector role in Prison Service', *Financial Times*, 30 May.

Byers, S. (2003) Speech at the Social Market Foundation: PPPs and PFI, 3 June, www. smf.co.uk/byers.html

Camp, S.D. and Gaes, G.G. (2001) *Growth and quality of US private prisons: Evidence from a national survey*, Washington DC: Federal Bureau of Prisons, September.

Carter, P. (2003) *Managing offenders, reducing crime: A new approach*, London: Ministry of Justice.

CBI (Confederation of British Industry) (2002) *Improving public services through public private partnership. A CBI statement of intent*, London: CBI.

CBI (2003) *Competition: A catalyst for change in the prison service*, London: CBI.

CBI (2008) *Getting back on the straight and narrow: A better criminal justice system for all*, London: CBI.

Corby, S. (2002) 'On parole: Prison service industrial relations', *Industrial Relations Journal*, vol 33, no 4, pp 286–97.

Davies, R. and Freedland, M. (2007) *Towards a flexible labour market: Labour legislation and regulation since the 1990s*, Oxford: Oxford University Press.

De Silva, N., Cowell, P., Chinegwundoh, V., Mason, T., Maresh, J. and Williamson, K. (2007) *Prison population projections 2007–2014: England and Wales*, Ministry of Justice Statistical Bulletin, London: Ministry of Justice.

DLA MCG Consulting (2003) *Privately managed custodial services,* September, Liverpool: DLA MCG Consulting.

DLA MCG Consulting (2004) *Privately managed custodial services,* September, Liverpool: DLA MCG Consulting.

DLA MCG Consulting (2006) *Privately managed custodial services,* September, Liverpool: DLA MCG Consulting.

Foley, K. (1994) 'The lessons of market testing: The experience of prison education', in K. Foley (ed) *Privatisation and market testing in the prison service,* London: Prison Reform Trust.

Fredman, S. and Morris, G. (1990) *The state as employer: Labour law in the public services,* London: Mansell.

Gaes, G., Scott, D., Nelson, J. and Saylor, W. (2004) *Measuring prison performance,* Walnut Creek, CA: Altamira Press.

Giddens, A. (2002) *Where now for New Labour?* Cambridge: Polity Press.

Greene, J. (2003) 'Lack of correctional services', in A. Coyle, A. Campbell and R. Neufeld (eds) *Capitalist punishment, prison privatisation and human rights,* London: Zed Books.

Harding, R. (1997) *Private prisons and public accountability,* Buckingham: Open University Press.

HMCIP (HM Chief Inspector of Prisons) (2001) *Report on a full announced inspection of HM Prison Manchester, 11–21 November,* www.homeoffice.gov.uk

HMCIP (2002a) *Report on a full announced inspection of HMP & YOI Ashfield, 1–5 July,* www.homeoffice.gov.uk

HMCIP (2002b) *Report on a full unannounced inspection of HMP Parc, 9–13 September,* www.homeoffice.gov.uk

HMCIP (2003a) *Report on a full announced inspection of HM Prison Dovegate, 31 March–4 April,* www.homeoffice.gov.uk

HMCIP (2003b) *Report on a full announced inspection of HM Prison Rye Hill, 16–20 June,* www.homeoffice.gov.uk

HM Prison Service (2003) *Annual Report and accounts April 2002–March 2003,* London: The Stationery Office.

HM Treasury (2003) *PFI: meeting the investment challenge,* London: HM Treasury.

Home Office (2004) *Reducing crime, changing lives: The government's plans for transforming the management of offenders,* London: Home Office.

House of Commons (Public Accounts Select Committee) (1999) *Thirty-third report: Managing sickness absence in the prison service,* London: The Stationery Office.

House of Commons PAC (2003) *Forty-ninth report: The operational performance of PFI prisons,* London: The Stationery Office.

House of Commons Treasury Select Committee (2004) *Sixth report: The 2004 Budget,* London: The Stationery Office.

IPPR (Institute of Public Policy Research) (2001) *Commission on Public Private Partnerships: Building better partnerships,* London: IPPR.

James, A.L., Bottomley, A.K., Liebling, A. and Clare, E. (1997) *Privatising prisons: Rhetoric and reality,* London: Sage Publications.

Kelly, G. (2000) *The new partnership agenda*, London: Institute of Public Policy Research.

King, R.D. and McDermott, K. (1989) *British prisons 1970-1987: The ever-deepening crisis*, British Journal of Criminology, vol 29, no 2, pp107-28.

Lewis, D. (1997) *Hidden agendas*, London: Hamish Hamilton.

Liebling, A. (2004) *Prisons and their moral performance*, Oxford: Oxford University Press.

Logan, C.H. (1987) *Privatising prisons: The moral case*, London: Adam Smith Institute.

Logan, C.H. (1990) *Private prisons*, New York: Oxford University Press.

Maltby, P. and Gosling, T. (2003) *Ending the 'two-tier' workforce*, London: Institute of Public Policy Research.

McDonald, D.C. (1994) 'Public imprisonment by private means', *British Journal of Criminology*, vol 34, special issue, pp 29–48.

McDonald, D.C. (ed) (1994) *Private prisons and the public interest*, New Brunswick: Rutgers University Press.

Miller, J. (2003) 'Worker rights in private prisons' in A. Coyle, A. Campbell and R. Neufeld (eds) *Capitalist punishment, prison privatisation and human rights*, London: Zed Books.

Moore, S. (1999) 'How contracting out city services impacts public employees', in P. Seidenstat (ed) *Contracting out government services*, Westport, CT: Praeger.

Morris, G.S. (2000) 'Employment in public services: The case for special treatment', *Oxford Journal of Legal Studies*, vol 20, no 2, pp 167-83.

Moyle, P. (1993) 'Privatisation of prisons in New South Wales and Queensland: A review of some key developments in Australia', *The Howard Journal of Criminal Justice*, vol 32, no 3, August, pp 231–50.

Nathan, S. (2003) 'Prison privatisation in Britain', in A. Coyle, A. Campbell and R. Neufeld (eds) *Capitalist punishment, prison privatisation and human rights*, London: Zed Books.

NAO (National Audit Office) (2003) *The operational performance of PFI prisons*, London: The Stationery Office.

NAO (2004) *The management of sickness absence in the prison service*, HC533, 19 May, London: The Stationery Office.

NOMS (National Offender Management Service) (2006) *Improving prison and probation services: Public value partnership*, London: Home Office.

Osborne, D. and Gaebler, T. (1992) *Reinventing government*, New York: Plume.

Parenti, C. (2003) 'Privatised problems: For profit incarceration in trouble' in A. Coyle, A. Campbell and R. Neufeld (eds) *Capitalist punishment, prison privatisation and human rights*, London: Zed Books.

Park, I. (2000) *Review of comparative costs and performance of privately and publicly operated prisons 1998–99*, issue 6/00, March, London: Home Office Research, Development and Statistics Directorate.

Pike, A. (1996) *In partnership, subject to contract*, London: Economic and Social Research Council.

Power, M. (1997) *The audit society: Rituals of verification*, Oxford: Oxford University Press.

PRT (Prison Reform Trust) (1994) *Private prison services in Australia*, briefing paper, London: PRT.

PRT (1996) *Privately managed prisons: At what cost?* January, London: PRT.

PSPRB (Prison Service Pay Review Body) (2003) *Second report on England and Wales*, Cm 5719, London: The Stationery Office.

PSPRB (2004) *Third report on England and Wales*, Cm 6129, London: The Stationery Office.

PSPRB (2005) *Fourth report on England and Wales*, Cm 6478, London: The Stationery Office.

PSPRB (2008) *Seventh report on England and Wales*, Cm 7325, London: The Stationery Office.

Rutherford, A. (1990) 'British penal policy and the idea of prison privatisation', in D.C. McDonald (ed) *Private prisons and the public interest*, New Brunswick: Rutgers University Press.

Ryan, M. (1994) 'Privatisation, corporate interest and the future shape and ethos of the prison service', in *Privatisation and market testing in the prison service*, London: Prison Reform Trust.

Ryan, M. (2003) *Penal policy and political culture in England and Wales*, Winchester: Waterside Press.

Ryan, M. and Ward, T. (1989) *Privatisation and the penal system*, Milton Keynes: Open University Press.

Sachdev, S. (2001) *Contracting culture: From CCT to PPPs*, London: Unison.

Schior, D. (1995) *Punishment for profit*, Thousand Oaks, CA: Sage.

Sherwood, B. (2005) 'Tories would use private sector for new jails', *Financial Times*, 8 February.

Sturgess, G. and Smith, B. (2006a) *Designing public service markets: The custodial sector as a case study*, London: The Serco Institute.

Sturgess, G. and Smith, B. (2006b) Designing value and quality in the custodial sector', in A. Milburn et al, *Private investment for public success*, London: The Policy Network.

Thompson, P. (2000) 'PPPs in criminal justice', *New Economy*, vol 7, no 3, September.

Tilt, R. (2005) Letter to the author, 12 April.

Timmins, N. (2002) 'Public sector pensions trail in shift from final salary', *Financial Times*, 18 February.

Willets, D. (1993) *The opportunities for private funding in the NHS*, Occasional Paper no 3, London: Social Market Foundation.

Wolff, R. (2004) 'The "efficiency" illusion', in E. Fullbrook (ed) *A guide to what's wrong with economics*, London: Anthem Press.

Young, P. (1987) *The prison cell: The start of a better approach to prison management*, London: Adam Smith Institute.

Reducing the use of custody as a sanction: a review of recent international experiences

7

Julian Roberts

How might a legislature reduce the use of custody as a sanction? Constraining rising (or reducing stable) prison populations remains a challenge confronting most western nations. It is now more than 20 years since the United Nations Standard Rules for Non-Custodial Measures[1] (the so-called 'Tokyo Rules') were adopted, the principal goal of which was to reduce the traditional reliance on imprisonment as a legal punishment. Throughout the 1990s, however, prison populations rose in many common law jurisdictions, particularly England and Wales and the US. The prison population in England and Wales grew by over 60% during the decade 1995–2005 (Ministry of Justice, 2007, p. 4). Similar correctional trends may be found elsewhere: A Home Office survey notes that prison populations rose in almost three-quarters of the countries included since the previous survey five years earlier (Walmsley, 2007). These trends are particularly disconcerting when one considers that crime rates, and hence the volume of offenders appearing before the courts, were stable or declining during much of this period (see Kershaw et al, 2008).

Purpose of chapter

In its recently published report, the Sentencing Commission Working Group (2008b) has concluded that a US-style sentencing commission, one which takes prison capacity into account when devising and revising its guidelines, is inappropriate for England and Wales. Others have taken a different view. Hough and Jacobson (2008) for example advocated creation of such a sentencing commission to help constrain the rising prison population in England and Wales. A sentencing commission is only one way of achieving this goal, however.

This chapter reviews other strategies which have been implemented or proposed to control or reduce the size of the prison population. It is worth noting that although many temporary and permanent sentencing commissions as well as ad hoc commissions of inquiry have been created across the common law world, none of these has conducted a systematic, evidence-based review of the effectiveness of different approaches to reducing the size of the prison population.[2] This chapter represents a small step towards identifying the components that make up a successful decarceration strategy. As will be seen, a diversity of strategies has been adopted in recent years.[3] I comment on the advantages – and some disadvantages – of different strategies. The discussion is restricted to remedial efforts that exist *within* the criminal justice system. A more radical – and potentially more effective – approach involves diverting cases away from the justice system in the first place. While such an approach would presumably focus primarily on less serious cases, these individuals can represent a significant proportion of the courts' caseload. For example, there is a growing movement promoting the use of criminal mediation (see Palmer, 1997).

I do not explore the utility of numerical guidelines such as those contained in the US-style sentencing grids, for two reasons. First, no other jurisdiction has adopted this approach to structuring judicial discretion.[4] Second, as noted, the Sentencing Commission Working Group has rejected adoption of a grid system for this jurisdiction. The Working Group's decision is consistent with views of almost all parties who made a submission to the Group's consultation paper (see Sentencing Commission Working Group, 2008c). In jurisdictions that employ a sentencing guidelines matrix (such as many American states) the size of the prison population can be reduced with relative ease simply by moving more offences into the community sanctions zone of the grid, or reducing the sentence lengths prescribed by the guidelines.

Matters are more complicated in common law countries that do not employ formal sentencing guidelines of this nature. Most of the strategies discussed here involve legislative intervention in the sphere of sentencing. It is a regrettable fact that legislatures around the world have proved reluctant to intervene in the sentencing process, preferring to leave the determination of sanction to judicial discretion, with very little guidance beyond the maximum penalty structure, or a small number of minimum sentences. I say that this is regrettable, for as O'Malley points out, 'the legislature has a vitally important role in prescribing punishments and other dispositions that are available to courts and the factors that may or should be taken into account [at sentencing]' (2000, p 450). Unfortunately, not all legislatures have accepted their responsibility in this respect. The chapter concludes by summarising the steps that may comprise a successful integrated strategy. One obvious feature of the international experience to date is that no jurisdiction has evolved an integrated approach to lowering the use of custody. Strategies have been implemented on an ad hoc basis, often in response to a sudden rise in the prison population. First, however, it is worth summarising trends with respect to the relative use of custody across jurisdictions.

Proportionate use of custody

There is considerable variation in the proportionate use of custody as a sanction, even between jurisdictions with comparable crime rates. For example, in Finland, only 7% of dispositions involve incarceration, compared with 28% in New Zealand, 35% in Canada and 61% at the state level in the US (see Roberts, 2004). This cross-jurisdictional variation is significant because it suggests that the use of imprisonment reflects attitudes to punishment as much as a judicial response to the seriousness of the crime problem. In other words, if Finland can tolerate a lower custody rate than many other jurisdictions, there is hope for other countries where imprisonment is more frequently imposed as a sanction.

Targeting offenders sentenced to brief periods of custody

In most western countries, a significant proportion of prison sentences is under six months in duration. For example, in Canada and Denmark, approximately nine prison terms out of 10 are less than six months. In France and Sweden over 60% of prison terms fall into this category (see Roberts, 2004, Table 2.4). O'Donnell reports that in Ireland almost half of the sentences of imprisonment are less than three months (1998, p 55). Similarly, in England and Wales, 60% of custodial sentences imposed in the Magistrates' courts in 2004 were three months or less, while over 90% were under six months (Home Office, 2005, Table 2.1). Offenders sentenced to short periods of custody seldom represent a threat to the community. In short, some of these offenders are prime candidates for community-based alternatives to imprisonment. However, since these offenders have been convicted of crimes that (presumably) meet the threshold for a custodial sentence, the substitute sanction must carry sufficient penal 'bite' to accomplish the objectives of sentencing, and to ensure an acceptable degree of community support. A community-based sanction that falls short of the penal equivalent of a term of custody will not be seen as an adequate replacement for a term of imprisonment.

Strategies to reduce the use of custody as a sanction

Statutory directions to sentencers regarding the use of imprisonment

The most obvious strategy to restrain the use of custody is simply to direct sentencers to use the sanction sparingly, with restraint. Although this approach has proved ineffective in England and Wales at containing the rising prison population, it may have proved more effective elsewhere. For example, the custody rate has remained relatively stable in Canada since the principle of restraint was codified in 1996. In fact, the most common attempt to restrict the use of custody has been to place certain principles on a statutory footing, of which restraint regarding the use of custody as a sanction is the most important. The legislature needs to send a clear message to courts that custody should be imposed only when it is satisfied that no other sanction will adequately promote the objectives of sentencing. Placing the principle of parsimony or restraint on a statutory footing serves a dual purpose. First, it should serve to prevent judges from incarcerating offenders unless no community-based sanction is deemed sufficient. This of course is the primary function of the principle. However, if the legislature places its imprimatur on the principle of restraint it will be hard for the same assembly to introduce mandatory sentences of imprisonment at a later point, as these sentences clearly violate the principle and exacerbate the problem of a rising prison population.[5]

(i) Examples of the Principle of Restraint regarding the use of custody

The principle of restraint with respect to the use of custody has been placed on a statutory footing in many common law countries. For example, in Canada sections 718.2(d) and (e) of the Criminal Code state that:

> An offender should not be deprived of liberty, if less restrictive sanctions may be appropriate in the circumstances; and all available sanctions other than imprisonment that are reasonable in the circumstances should be considered for all offenders, with particular attention to the circumstances of aboriginal offenders.

In England and Wales, the 2003 Criminal Justice Act reaffirmed the importance of restraint in sentencing, by promoting the principle of proportionality. In determining whether a custodial sentence should be imposed, crime seriousness is established as a guiding consideration: Section 152 (2) of the Act states that:

> The court must not pass a custodial sentence unless it is of the opinion that the offence, or the combination of the offence and one or more offences associated with it, was so serious that neither a fine alone nor a community sentence can be justified for the offence.

Similarly, with respect to the length of a discretionary custodial sentence, Section 153 (2) of the Act states that:

> Subject to sections 51A(2) of the Firearms Act 1968 (c.27), sections 110(2) and 111(2) of the Sentencing Act and sections 227(2) and 228(2) of this Act, the custodial sentence must be for the shortest term (not exceeding the permitted maximum) that in the opinion of the court is commensurate with the seriousness of the offence, or the combination of the offence and one or more of the offences associated with it.

Other countries have also recently placed the principle of restraint on a statutory footing. The language used in the New Zealand statute is particularly directive. Courts are instructed that:

> The court must not impose a sentence of imprisonment unless it is satisfied that:
> (a) a sentence is being imposed for all or any of the [statutory] purposes [of sentencing]; and
> (b) those purposes cannot be achieved by a sentence other than imprisonment; and
> (c) no other sentence would be consistent with the application of the principles [of sentencing]. (section 16(2) of the 2002 Sentencing Act)

Thus codifying a general direction to sentencers regarding the parsimonious use of custody represents the most frequently adopted attempt to curb the size of the prison population. The principle of restraint is clear enough, but this step alone will prove insufficient, otherwise the problem of rising custody rates would be easily solved. Indeed, the experience in England and Wales illustrates this point well. The restraint provision was introduced in the 1991 Criminal Justice Act. However, between 1991 and 2001, the custody rate in that jurisdiction rose significantly, as did the size of the custodial population (see Hough et al, 2003).

(ii) Placing the principle of proportionality on a statutory footing

Privileging the principle of proportionality may also be of assistance in constraining admissions to prison. By placing desert-based limits on the severity of the sentence that may be imposed, this principle will help to restrict the use of incarceration by preventing judges from employing harsher sentences (that is, more and longer terms of custody) in an attempt to curb rising crime rates.

Many jurisdictions, including Canada, England and Wales, Finland and New Zealand have placed the principle of proportionality on a statutory footing or have proposed to do so. For example, in Canada, Parliament has designated the following principle as fundamental: 'A sentence must be proportionate to the gravity of the offence and the degree of responsibility of the offender.' The Finnish statute is comparable: 'The punishment shall be measured so that it is in just proportion to the harm and risk involved in the offence and to the culpability of the offender manifested in the offence.'[6] Under the proposals made by the Law Commission in South Africa retributive sentencing is established by means of the first two principles that read as follows: (1) 'Sentences must be proportionate to the seriousness of the offence committed, relative to sentences imposed for other categories or sub-categories of offences'; and (2) 'The seriousness of the offence committed is determined by the degree of harmfulness or risked harmfulness of the offence and the degree of culpability of the offender for the offence committed.' (South African Law Commission, 2000). Thus proportionality is established as the primordial consideration in determining sentence severity.

Restrain sentence escalation in response to reoffending

Judges sometimes follow what might be termed a sentencing strategy of 'penal escalation'. If an offender receives a non-custodial sanction and is subsequently reconvicted, courts tend to gravitate towards a more severe disposition on the second or subsequent occasion. This is a form of recidivist sentencing premium; the judicial logic underlying the strategy is that if a community-based sanction did not 'work' on the first occasion (as evidenced by the offender's reappearance before the court), perhaps custody should be imposed on the second. The application of this logic is likely to violate proportionality considerations and also to increase the number of admissions to custody.

An offender should be committed to custody only if the current offence is sufficiently serious that no other sanction could be justified. An offender should not be denied consideration of a non-custodial sentence simply because he received such a sentence on a previous sentencing occasion. Restricting this tendency by courts represents a way of restraining the number of prison sentences imposed. The Canadian youth justice legislation serves as a useful model in this respect. A provision in the Canadian Youth Criminal Justice Act is intended to discourage judges from escalating the severity of the sentence in response to subsequent offending. Section 39(4) states that:

> The previous imposition of a particular non-custodial sentence on a young person does not preclude a youth justice court from imposing the same or any other non-custodial sentence for another offence.

While s. 39(4) does not prohibit judges from following the 'step principle' logic at sentencing, the provision makes it clear that the same alternative may be imposed on separate occasions. If the intention of 'stepping up' the tariff is to reflect the offender's status as a repeat offender, this may in many cases be accomplished by making the community sentence more onerous.

Establish statutory criteria for the imposition of custodial sentences

A more effective way of constraining the number of offenders sent to prison consists of the creation of specific criteria that must be fulfilled before a term of custody may be imposed. Few jurisdictions have gone so far as to codify such conditions. However, in Canada, the 2003 youth justice statute does exactly this. According to section 39 of the Youth Criminal Justice Act, a youth court may send a young offender to prison only if one or more of four criteria are met:

> A youth justice court shall not commit a young offender to custody unless the young offender has:
> * committed a violent offence; or
> * failed to comply with previous non-custodial sentences; or
> * committed an offence for which an adult is liable for a term of imprisonment greater than 2 years and who has a history that indicates a pattern of findings of guilt; or
> * 'in exceptional circumstances', the young offender has committed an indictable offence, the circumstances of which mean that the imposition of a non-custodial sanction would be inconsistent with the purpose and principles of sentencing.

The youth justice reforms were introduced in Canada in 2003 (see Bala and Roberts, 2006). Since then, there has been a significant decline in the volume of young persons admitted to custody. In the first two years following implementation, the average number of young offenders in prison declined by 60% (Calverly, 2007). Although these criteria apply only to young offenders, there is little reason why criteria could not be created to restrict the imprisonment of adult offenders in a similar fashion.[7]

Requiring reasons for sentence, or for the imposition of a custodial term

A weaker approach to restricting the use of custody consists of requiring judges to provide reasons for sentence. Many countries have created a statutory obligation on judges to provide reasons for the sentences that they impose. Such a requirement facilitates appellate review of sentencing decisions and is in the interests of the administration of justice.[8] However, requiring judges to justify the imposition of a term of custody may also help to reduce the use of custody; judges may be less likely to impose a sentence if the use of this disposition requires specific justification. Once again the Youth Criminal Justice Act in Canada provides a useful illustration. Section s. 39(9) of the Act creates a duty for youth court judges who impose a term of custody to provide reasons why 'it has determined that a non-custodial sentence is not adequate' to achieve the purpose of sentencing ascribed to the youth court system.

Abolition of short sentences of imprisonment

A number of commentators have proposed abolishing all sentences of custody under a certain limit, for example six months.[9] The Scottish Prisons Commission recently proposed a statutory bar against the imposition of terms of custody under six months, unless one or more of a limited number of conditions are met (Scottish Prisons Commission, 2008, p 39).[10] Moreover, if a court were to pass a sentence of six months or less, it would have to state why only a custodial sentence could be imposed in such a case (p 39).

There are a number of objections to such a policy. First, a strategy of this kind may easily backfire. Judges may decide, in light of the seriousness of the offence, that a term of custody is necessary. Then, having arrived at this determination, the court would be compelled to impose a six-month term. To the extent that this logic is followed, the average duration of custodial terms would rise, as some cases formerly attracting a sentence of a couple of months would now jump to the mandatory six month minimum.[11] This proposal thereby might have the effect of creating a form of mandatory minimum sentence of imprisonment. In addition, the logic underlying a prohibition of short prison sentences is questionable. Imagine amending the fine provisions by creating a minimum amount, requiring courts to impose a fine of, say, at least £1,000. A reform of this nature would make little sense to the community. If a particular disposition carries some penal value it should do so at all stages of a continuum.[12]

The proposal to eliminate short prison sentences is also founded upon an assumption not shared by all, namely that the only offenders who should be sent to prison are those who pose a threat to the security of the public – violent or sexual offences in the context of the Scottish Prisons Commissions proposal. There is an argument that some offences are sufficiently serious as to require the incarceration of the offender even if he or she is no longer a threat, or even if they are unlikely to reoffend. Consider a sadly common offence these days: defrauding the elderly. The full impact of economic crimes on elderly persons – often women living alone or with a female companion – is only now being fully appreciated by the courts. The psychological harm created by such crimes is high, and the offenders who target such persons thereby display a level of moral turpitude that many people would argue demands a term of imprisonment. But the imposition, say, of a three-month prison term in such cases would be impossible under the Scottish proposal.

Finally, it is worth noting in this context that the Australian Law Reform Commission recently completed a comprehensive review of sentencing reform options. The abolition of sentences of less than six months was one of the reforms examined, but ultimately rejected by the Commission. The Commission cited evidence from Western Australia that the abolition of short sentences may have perverse consequences, in that offenders would receive longer sentences than would otherwise have been imposed (see Australian Law Reform Commission, 2005, pp 236–7). Placing restrictions on the ability of a court to impose a short term of custody may therefore not be a wise strategy for reducing the prison population. A better solution can be found in Germany, where all prison sentences under six months must be suspended unless the court is of the opinion that the rehabilitative needs of the offender require his or her immediate imprisonment (see Albrecht, 2002). A more general approach might be to require the suspension of all short sentences unless it would be contrary to the interests of justice to do so.

Limit the impact of previous convictions at sentencing

Any sentencing system that imposes significantly harsher sentences on recidivists will have a problem with rising prison populations. Some scholars question the practice of assigning any weight to previous convictions at sentencing. Retributive theorists such as Fletcher (1982) argue that previous convictions should not be counted against the defendant as they do not affect his or her level of culpability for the offence or the seriousness of the offence. Others such as von Hirsch (for example, von Hirsch, 1985) propose a very limited use: first offenders or those with a small number of priors should receive a discount, but once the 'first offender' discount has been exhausted, additional convictions should not increase the severity of sentence.

It is unrealistic to expect the sentencing system to totally or largely ignore an offender's criminal antecedents. Indeed, all sentencing systems consider an offender's prior record (see Roberts, 2008), but for the purposes of reducing the prison population it is necessary to prevent criminal history from having a disproportionate influence on sentencing outcomes. A significant proportion of offenders appearing before the courts have criminal records; if each previous conviction is weighed again at each subsequent sentencing hearing, incarceration is the likely result.

The 2003 Criminal Justice Act increases the influence of previous convictions at sentencing. Thus section 143(1) of the Act stipulates that:

> In considering the seriousness of an offence ('the current offence') committed by an offender who has one or more previous convictions, the court must treat each previous conviction as an aggravating factor if (in the case of that conviction) the court considers that it can reasonably be so treated having regard, in particular to (a) the nature of the offence to which the conviction relates and its relevance to the current offence, and (b) the time that has elapsed since the conviction.

In this way, if the court considers it relevant, each previous conviction will inflate the quantum of punishment imposed – in short, cumulative sentencing. However, some constraint must be placed on sentencers, or previous convictions will become more important than the seriousness of the crime. And, since many offenders have previous convictions, the result will be an increase in prison populations as institutions fill up with recidivists (see von Hirsch and Roberts, 2004). In this respect the sentencing reform proposals advanced by the Irish Law Reform Commission and the South African Law Commission offer a useful model. The Law Reform Commission of Ireland took the position that 'although it may be justifiable to take account of the offender's previous criminal record ... the sentence should be kept in proportion to the seriousness of the current offence(s)' (Law Reform Commission of Ireland, 1993, p 384). The South African proposals state that: 'the presence or absence of relevant previous convictions may be used to modify the sentence proportionate to the seriousness of the offence to *a moderate degree*' (South African Law Commission, 2000; S. 3(4), emphasis added). This phrase would require clarification from appellate courts; however, it does introduce a clear constraint upon the degree to which the severity of a sentence can be increased to reflect the offender's previous convictions. No such constraint exists under the Criminal Justice Act, where each prior conviction must aggravate sentence severity, as long as it is considered recent and relevant.[13]

Realign and lower all maximum penalties

Another way of influencing sentencers involves a revision of the maximum penalty structure. Little attention is ever paid to the statutory maxima – either by judges or legislators. Courts seldom have need to consider the statutory maximum when determining sentence simply because the maxima in most common law countries derive from the 19th century, and no longer correspond to the seriousness of the offences for which they may be imposed (Advisory Council on the Penal System,

1978). The vast majority of custodial sentences are much shorter than the statutory maximum.

If all the statutory maxima were lowered from their current levels this may result in shorter terms of imprisonment, and this in turn would have a significant impact on the prison population. In addition, since the reform would affect all offences simultaneously, proportionality in sentencing would be preserved. But how effective is this likely to be as a strategy to reduce the size of the prison population? The evidence is far from promising. In other jurisdictions, trial court sentencing practices have not been affected by changes to the maximum penalty structure.

In its consultation paper the Sentencing Commission in England and Wales provided sentencing statistics for two offences before and after Parliament had reduced the maximum penalty (Sentencing Commission Working Group, 2008a). In one case, a reduction in the maximum sentence for theft did appear to trigger a reduction in the average sentence length for this offence. With respect to the other offence (commercial burglary), the reduction from 14 to 10 years had no discernible impact on subsequent sentencing practices (see Sentencing Commission Working Group, 2008a, pp 25–6). Finally, it would also prove difficult to sell this approach to the public, parliamentarians or the judiciary. It will be recalled that in 1979 the Advisory Council on the Maximum penalty structure recommended lowering the maximum penalties to the 90th percentile custodial sentence. The proposal was never adopted, in large measure as a result of judicial opposition.

Develop Alternate Forms of Custody or Alternative Sanctions

As Vaughan noted, in relation to juvenile offenders, 'the most popular way of reducing the incarceration rate is to provide more non-custodial alternatives' (Vaughan, 2000, p 14). The same can be said for the sentencing of adults. An obvious way to decrease the use of imprisonment as a sanction is simply to offer judges more sentencing options in the hope that one will prove an acceptable substitute for imprisonment. This strategy has been embraced by many jurisdictions (Walmsley, 2003). However, simply increasing the range of sanctions available to sentencing courts has not to date accomplished the anticipated reductions in prison populations. One limitation on alternatives to imprisonment is that they are not as severe, or are not perceived to be as severe as a term of custody. This limits the extent to which alternative sanctions can be substituted for terms of imprisonment. The development of tougher community-based sanctions is one response to this problem.

(i) Home alone: home confinement sanctions

The search for more punitive community-based sanctions has led to the creation of another variation on institutional imprisonment: community custody. Home confinement, (also referred to as community custody) is capable of fulfilling many penal objectives, some punitive, some reintegrative. They include: (i) isolating the offender; (ii) rupturing his or her criminogenic associations; (iii) promoting rehabilitation by allowing the offender to maintain community links. Only the first of these objectives is easily accomplished in prison. Home confinement regimes vary widely – some are quite punitive in nature, others more resemble a term of probation with a curfew or house arrest condition (see Roberts, 2004, for a review of different international models). As well, the ambit of these sanctions varies considerably. Usually, the sanction is used to replace relatively brief periods of institutional confinement. Three jurisdictions offer important lessons with respect to this strategy.

(a) Finland

Finland remains the jurisdiction that has employed community custody sentences to the greatest extent. Called conditional imprisonment, it has proved a success in that jurisdiction, and has played an important role in reducing the use of incarceration as a sanction. Over the past 50 years, the volume of conditional sentences imposed in Finland has increased dramatically. In 1950, conditional imprisonment accounted for 2,812 sentences, under a third of all sentences of imprisonment. In 2000, 13,974 such dispositions were imposed, representing just under two thirds of all prison sentences (Lappi-Seppala, 2002). The experience in Finland therefore demonstrates the power of community custody to reduce the size of the prison population.

(b) New Zealand

In contrast, New Zealand employs a far more restrictive and modest home confinement sanction. Assignment to home detention in New Zealand requires a two-step approval process involving the judiciary and an administrative body. The consequence is that a small minority of eligible offenders are released to serve their sentences at home. Only some offenders will be eligible for home confinement. Of these, only a minority will be granted leave to apply, and many will ultimately be turned down by the parole board. In one study less than one-third of prisoners who applied for home confinement had been granted release to the programme (Gibbs and King, 2003). An even smaller percentage of all prisoners within the range of sentence length will serve part of the sentence in the programme. In 2001, only 10% of offenders sentenced to a prison sentence of two years or less (and therefore within the ambit of the home detention regime) were actually released to serve their sentences at home (Spier, 2002). The experience in New Zealand demonstrates the importance of allowing the ambit of this sanction to be relatively broad, if any significant impact on prison populations is to be achieved.

(c) Canada

Canada is the most recent jurisdiction to introduce a community custody sanction (in 1996).[14] In Canada, the home confinement sentence (known as a conditional sentence of imprisonment) may replace[15] most sentences of custody of up to two years in duration. This embraces fully 96% of custodial sentences imposed. This wide ambit of application is a double-edged sword. On the one hand, it permits the sanction to replace a large number of terms of institutional imprisonment, thereby increasing the decarceration effect of the sentence. On the other hand, it permits courts to impose a term of custody for crimes of violence serious enough to justify a lengthy (by Canadian standards) term of imprisonment. This does not often happen, but when it does, media coverage is very negative.[16]

This image problem aside, research has demonstrated the effectiveness of the Canadian home confinement sentence in reducing the volume of admissions to custody. Pre and post implementation analyses of admission statistics demonstrate that within three years of creation of the sanction, a 13% reduction in admissions was directly attributable to the new sanction. This represents about 55,000 offenders who served their sentences of imprisonment at home, rather than in a correctional facility. In addition, the success rate – the proportion of orders completed without a violation of conditions – appears relatively high. Over the first four years of the new sanction, approximately four orders out of five terminated without violation of the conditions (Roberts, 2004).

(ii) Intermittent custody

If an offender must be committed to custody, there are powerful arguments for allowing him or her to serve it on the weekend. Almost all common law jurisdictions allow courts to impose intermittent terms of imprisonment according to which offenders serve their sentences on consecutive weekends. As with home confinement, intermittent detention usually carries a relatively low statutory limit, with the result that only offenders sentenced to relatively short periods of custody are permitted to serve the sentence on weekends. A typical ceiling is 90 days, found in a number of common law jurisdictions. Intermittent prisoners create additional demands for correctional facilities, as they are not housed, or should not be housed, with the regular prison population. This means the construction or conversion of 'weekend facilities'. Nevertheless, these facilities are cheaper to run than conventional prisons. In addition, the benefits to the offender – and his or her family – are striking. Intermittent custody prisoners are able to maintain employment and the secondary impact of the sentence on dependants is greatly mitigated. Research reported by

Penfold, Hunter and Hough (2006) found generally positive outcomes: almost all intermittent custody prisoners were able to maintain their employment. Intermittent custody was introduced in England and Wales by the 2003 Criminal Justice Act, although it has yet to be fully implemented.

(iii) Other alternative sentencing options[17]

Little scholarly attention has been paid to other possible ways of censuring offenders without resort to custody. Restrictions on an offender's lifestyle may also offer a means of avoiding the imposition of a brief term of custody. In most countries people who accumulate a number of driving-related convictions are subject to mandatory licence suspensions. The link between the offence – culpable driving – and the sanction (suspension of driving privileges) is clear. But there is no reason why a number of privileges of citizenship or residency should not be temporarily withdrawn as a penal response to other forms of offending. These restrictions could include the ability to travel (suspension of passport) or the ability to drive. Weekend curfews are another restriction on an individual's lifestyle, and may be particularly appropriate for younger offenders. Restrictions such as these would have a clear, punitive impact on the offender, and may well form part of a community-based sentence. If the number and intrusiveness of the lifestyle restrictions were calibrated to reflect proportionality considerations, they could play a useful role in helping to reduce the level of admissions to custody.

Periodic amnesties of prisoners

Some jurisdictions employ sporadic, one-time conditional release initiatives to reduce the size of the prison population. In France, general amnesties are periodically granted to mark an event of national significance. Amnesties (known as 'executive remissions') have also been used in South Africa to relieve intolerable prison conditions due to overcrowding. For example, in 2005, a special remission of sentence was granted to prisoners serving sentences of imprisonment for non-violent offences. This resulted in the release of approximately 32,000 individuals and reduced the total prison population from 187,000 to 155,000 (Giffard and Muntingh, 2006, p 32). This is certainly a rapid means of reducing the prison population – large numbers of prisoners can be released practically overnight. Although they can be effective in this respect, such amnesties can provoke public opposition, and undermine principled sentencing (see Pete, 1998, for discussion in the South African context). They are therefore not a reasonable substitute for more permanent and principled approaches to reducing the number of prisoners.

Reducing the proportion of time spent in prison

A more systematic strategy consists of increasing the proportion of a sentence of imprisonment that may be served in the community on parole. Some jurisdictions regulate their prison populations by increasing the number of prisoners released on parole, or accelerating the parole eligibility date with the result that more prisoners are released, and at an earlier point in the sentence. When parole cuts deeply into a sentence of imprisonment, however, a number of problems arise. First, public opposition is provoked, as members of the public question the meaning of a term of custody if the offender is released into the community after having served only one-third of the sentence. Second, proportionality in sentencing will be undermined. When reviewing parole applications, parole authorities consider the threat to the community and the possible benefit to the prisoner of release on parole. Crime seriousness and offender culpability are not generally among the criteria for granting parole. Sentences that conform to proportionality considerations at the time of sentencing can become quite different when the amount of time served in prison is considered.[18]

Importance of promoting public and professional confidence in alternatives

Attempts to address the problem of a high prison population must be broadly acceptable to the community; otherwise criticism of the courts will intensify still further. Some proposals to reduce the use of custody will be more acceptable to the community than others. For example, ad hoc strategies such as prison amnesties or the unprincipled use of early release schemes would undoubtedly antagonise the public and fuel the perception that the justice system is too lenient or out of touch with community values. A MORI opinion poll conducted in 2006 asked a sample of the British public whether they supported or opposed a number of strategies to deal with the high prison population. Over half the sample opposed sending fewer people to prison, whereas approximately three-quarters of the sample endorsed the option of building more prisons (Duffy et al. 2007, p 51). However, this finding should be interpreted with care. It should not be taken as evidence of knee-jerk punitiveness on the part of the public. When the same polling firm asked members of the public to choose the most effective way of reducing crime, 'putting more offenders in prison' was the least popular option, supported by one respondent in 10 (Duffy et al. 2007, p 54). The public see clear limits on the effectiveness of incarceration as a crime control strategy.

Ultimately, promoting the use of alternatives and reducing the number of admissions to custody requires more than amendments to the statutory sentencing framework or the creation of additional non-custodial sentencing options. It also necessitates an effort to educate the public about the fiscal, penological, and humanitarian benefits of community sentences, as well the limitations on imprisonment as a criminal sanction.

It is a regrettable reality that when asked about sentencing, or about the sentence that is most appropriate in a specific case, the public around the world first think about imprisonment. Although custody is the sanction that comes most readily to mind, it is also the one with which people are least familiar. Most members of the public know little about prison conditions, and underestimate the true severity of a sentence of imprisonment. A review of public opinion surveys demonstrates that this is true around the world in all countries in which public opinion polls have explored this issue (Roberts and Hough, 2005a). This view of prison conditions has an inflationary effect on public expectations of the sentencing process: if prison life is relatively easy, a sentence such as six months in prison will not be seen as a severe penalty.

Public opinion research has demonstrated remarkable commonalities with respect to criminal justice. Polls conducted in countries as diverse as Britain, Barbados, South Africa and New Zealand reveal that the public around the world share a number of common attitudes regarding crime and criminal justice. Many of these can have an indirect effect on sentencers. For example, regardless of actual trends, most people believe that crime rates are constantly rising. This discrepancy between public perception and reality has emerged from studies conducted in many countries since the 1980s (see Roberts and Hough, 2005b).[19] The consequence of this misperception is likely to be pressure on courts to sentence more severely, as the public look to the sentencing process to address the problem.

Educating the public about crime rates and the nature of the sentencing process is therefore an important component in the struggle to reduce the use of custody. A public that perceives crime rates to be constantly rising, and that sees judges as routinely imposing lenient sentences, will create pressure on sentencers to impose more and longer prison terms. Public misperceptions will therefore become a cause of the problem.

Conclusion

The criminal justice system in England and Wales is clearly confronted with an urgent problem regarding the rising prison population. If the government heeds the advice of the Sentencing Commission Working Group and enhances significantly the statutory functions of a revamped Sentencing Guidelines Council, this is clearly a step in the right direction. Far more is needed, however, if the numbers of prisoners in this jurisdiction are to be brought down to the level of some other European jurisdictions. But as Hedderman notes in her contribution to this volume, 'there are no easy or quick fixes to constraining or reducing the size of the prison population'.

Any jurisdiction with the serious intention of reducing its prison population needs to adopt an integrated strategy, beginning with clear directions to sentencers regarding the necessity for restraint with respect to the use of custody. Statutory criteria for the imposition of a term of custody would also be useful in restricting the numbers of people sent to prison. Such legislative directions should be accompanied by a comprehensive guideline scheme which privileges, where appropriate, community sanctions and which provides clear guidance regarding the conditions under which committal to custody is appropriate. Attention also needs to be paid to the criminal justice response when offenders fail to comply with the terms of a community penalty. One of the principal causes of the current increase in the prison population in England and Wales is the rise in admissions for breach of conditions. The system needs to strike a balance: An indulgent response will encourage non-compliance and undermine the public image of community sanctions. On the other hand, a zero or near-zero level of tolerance of breach will lead to large numbers of people being admitted to custody for breach of an order rather than for the seriousness of their criminal conduct. In addition, governments should also consider repealing mandatory sentences of imprisonment. These sentences increase the size of the prison population for the specified offences and also have an indirect inflationary effect on sentences for other offences (see Giffard and Muntingh, 2006). Finally, these steps should be accompanied by community engagement, to promote professional and community support, without which the most carefully conceived penal strategy is doomed to failure.

Notes

[1] UN Document A/RES/45/110.

[2] I do not take up some proposals that have yet to be fully developed as a strategy. For example, consultees to the Sentencing Commission Working Group advocated greater use of discretion by probation officers regarding recall for technical breaches (see Sentencing Commission Working Group, 2008c, p 38). Nor do I deal with the suggestion that foreign prisoners – who account for approximately 13% of the total prison population – be deported (see House of Commons Committee of Public Accounts, 2006, p 7).

[3] The focus here is on the use of incarceration as a sanction; I do not address the problem of remand detention in part because pre-trial detention has not played a significant role in the rise of the prison population in England and Wales (see Jacobson et al, 2008). However, in some countries such as Italy and Belgium, substantial reductions in the prison population can be achieved by reducing the number of accused denied bail. For example, remand prisoners account for over half the prison population in Italy and almost half the prison population of Belgium (see Jacobson et al, 2008, p 26).

[4] In November 2000, Western Australia introduced legislation to adopt a sentencing matrix, although the legislation was never proclaimed into law.

[5] This is the theory at least; in reality matters do not always follow this path. For example, the Canadian Parliament codified the principle of restraint in 1996 yet

created a series of mandatory minimum sentences of imprisonment a year later, and more have been added since then.

[6] Criminal Code, Chapter 6, section 1, para 1 (see Lappi-Seppala, 2002).

[7] It may be harder, however, to convince legislatures to introduce strict criteria for the imposition of custody for adults since there is general recognition that imprisonment is more harmful for juveniles than for adult prisoners.

[8] It is also important that victims, offenders and other interested parties fully understand the reasons underlying a particular sentencing decision.

[9] Six months encompasses the vast majority of sentences of custody in most western jurisdictions. In Scotland for example, the Scottish Prisons Commission reports that in 2005/06 over four-fifths of all custodial sentences were six months or less in duration.

[10] The conditions which can give rise to a term of under six months are actually quite numerous and include the following: the presence of violent or sexual offences that raise concerns about serious harm; when the offence was committed while the offender was on bail; when the offender is already subject to a community supervision sentence or has failed in the past to comply with community or conditional sentences; when the offender is subject to a release licence; when the offender does not consent to the rehabilitative elements of a community supervision sentence; if the offender is serving a sentence of custody (see Scottish Prisons Commission, 2008, p 39).

[11] If there was a clear increase in the number of six-month sentences, this could be taken as evidence of courts moving up to the minimum, where previously they may have imposed, say, a sentence of 90 days.

[12] See discussion in Brodeur and Roberts (2001). For research pointing to an increase in the severity of sentences when judges are constrained to give at least six months of incarceration (see Kuhn, 1994).

[13] Other ways of mitigating the extent to which consideration of priors increases the size of the prison population is to allow offenders to counter the enhanced blameworthiness ascribed to them as a result of their previous convictions. Efforts at desistance, for example, should be weighed in the defendant's favour at sentencing, even if his or her presence before the court demonstrates that these efforts failed (see Roberts, 2008 for further discussion).

[14] The Scottish Prisons Commission has recommended the creation of a conditional sentence for that jurisdiction (see Scottish Prisons Commission, 2008, p 40).

[15] There are other criteria that must be fulfilled before a court can impose this sentence. Imposition of the sentence must be consistent with the codified purpose and principles of sentencing; the offence must not be one that carries a minimum term of imprisonment (few such crimes exist in Canada) and the court must be confident that the offender does not represent a threat to the community (see Roberts, 2004).

[16] The adverse publicity associated with the imposition of this sanction in a relatively small number of serious personal injury offences was an important factor in the government's recent decision to introduce restrictions to the ambit of the sanction (see Roberts, 2006).

[17] Restrictions on space prevent a more thorough discussion of the proposal but forfeiture of property is also worthy of greater consideration as an alternative to a brief period of imprisonment. Fines are often hard to collect, and some offenders ultimately choose to spend brief periods in custody rather than pay off a significant fine. Seizing assets is a more direct way of enriching the state, assuming that third parties do not suffer in the process.

[18] See discussion of this issue in the report of the Canadian Sentencing Commission (Canadian Sentencing Commission, 1987).

[19] The latest statistics from the 2007/08 British Crime Survey reveal that approximately two-thirds of the public believe that crime rates across the country had increased over the previous two years (Kershaw et al, 2008, p 117).

References

Advisory Council on the Penal System (1978) *Sentences of imprisonment: A review of maximum penalties. Report of the Advisory Council on the Penal System*, London: HMSO.

Albrecht, H.-J. (2002) 'Community sanctions in the Federal Republic of Germany', in H.-J. Albrecht and A. van Kalmthout (eds) *Community sanctions and measures in Europe and North America*, Freiburg: Edition Iuscrim.

Australian Law Reform Commission (2005) *Same crime, same time: Sentencing of federal offenders*, Report 103. Sydney: Australian Law Reform Commission.

Bala, N. and Roberts, J.V. (2006) 'Canada's juvenile justice system: Promoting community-based responses to youth crime,' in J. Junger-Tas and S. Decker (eds) *International handbook of juvenile justice*, Dordrecht: Springer Publications.

Brodeur, J.P. and Roberts, J.V. (2001) 'Taking justice seriously', *Canadian Criminal Law Review*, vol 7, pp 77–92.

Calverly, C. (2007) 'Youth custody and community services in Canada, 2004/05', *Juristat*, vol 27, no 2.

Canadian Sentencing Commission (1987) *Sentencing reform: A Canadian approach*, Ottawa: Supply and Services Canada.

Duffy, B., Wake, R., Burrows, T. and Bremner, P. (2007) *Closing the gaps: Crime and public perceptions*, London: MORI.

Fletcher, G. (1982) 'The recidivist premium', *Criminal Justice Ethics*, vol 1, pp 54–9.

Gibbs, A. and King, D. (2003) 'Home detention with electronic monitoring: The New Zealand experience', *Criminal Justice*, vol 3, pp 199–211.

Giffard, C. and Muntingh, L. (2006) *The effect of sentencing on the size of the South African prison population*, Report 3, Newlands: Open Society Foundation for South Africa.

Home Office (2005) *Sentencing statistics 2004*, London: Home Office, Research, Development and Statistics Directorate.

Hough, M. and Jacobson, J. (2008) *Creating a sentencing commission for England and Wales: An opportunity to address the prisons crisis*, London: Prison Reform Trust.

Hough, M., Jacobson, J. and Millie, A. (2003) *The decision to imprison: Sentencing and the prison population*, London: The Prison Reform Trust.

House of Commons Committee of Public Accounts (2006) *National Offender Management Service: Dealing with increased numbers in custody*, London: Stationery Office.

Jacobson, J., Roberts, J.V., Hough, M. and Player, E. (2008) *Remanded in custody: A review of remand decision-making in England and Wales*, London: Nuffield Foundation.

Kershaw, C., Nicholas, S. and Walker, A. (2008) *Crime in England and Wales 2007/08*, Home Office Statistical Bulletin 07/08, London: Home Office, www.homeoffice. gov.uk/rds/pdfs08/hosb0708.pdf

Kuhn, A. (1994) 'What can we do about prison overcrowding?' *European Journal of Criminal Policy and Research*, vol 2, pp 101–33.

Lappi-Seppala, T. (2002) *The principle of proportionality in the Finnish sentencing system*, www.optula.om.fi/uploads/0baxiwlo9o.pdf

Law Reform Commission of Ireland (1993) *Consultation paper on sentencing*, Dublin: The Law Reform Commission.

Ministry of Justice (2007) *Story of the prison population: 1995–2007*, London: Ministry of Justice.

O'Donnell, I. (1998) 'Challenging the punitive obsession', *Irish Criminal Law Journal*, vol 8, pp 51–66.

O'Malley, T. (2000) *Sentencing law and practice*, Dublin: Sweet and Maxwell.

Palmer, R. (1997) 'Justice in whose interests? A proposal for institutionalised mediation in the criminal justice system', *South African Journal of Criminal Justice*, vol 10, pp 33–45.

Penfold, C., Hunter, G. and Hough, M. (2006) 'The intermittent custody pilot: A descriptive study', *Findings, No 280*, London: Home Office, Research, Development and Statistics Directorate.

Pete, S. (1998) 'The politics of imprisonment in the aftermath of South Africa's first democratic election', *South African Journal of Criminal Justice*, vol 11, pp 51–83.

Roberts, J.V. (2004) *The virtual prison: Community custody and the evolution of imprisonment*, Cambridge: Cambridge University Press.

Roberts, J.V. (2006) 'Reforming conditional sentencing: Evaluating recent legislative proposals', *Criminal Law Quarterly*, vol 52, pp 18–35.

Roberts, J.V. (2008) *Punishing persistent offenders*, Oxford: Oxford University Press.

Roberts, J.V. and Hough, M. (2005a) 'The state of the prisons: Exploring public knowledge and opinion', *The Howard Journal of Criminal Justice*, vol 44, no 3, pp 286–307.

Roberts, J.V. and Hough, M. (2005b) *Understanding public attitudes to criminal justice*, Maidenhead: Open University Press.

Scottish Prisons Commission (2008) *Scotland's choice: Report of the Scottish Prisons Commission*, Edinburgh: Scottish Prisons Commission.

Sentencing Commission Working Group (2008a) *Consultation document*, London: Ministry of Justice.

Sentencing Commission Working Group (2008b) *Sentencing guidelines in England and Wales: An evolutionary approach*, London: Ministry of Justice.

Sentencing Commission Working Group (2008c) *A summary of responses to the Sentencing Commission Working Group's consultation paper*, London: Ministry of Justice.

South African Law Commission (2000) *Sentencing (A new sentencing framework)*, Discussion Paper 91 (Project 82), www.law.wits.ac.za/salc/discussion/proposal

Spier, P. (2002) *Conviction and sentencing of offenders in New Zealand: 1992–2001*, Wellington: New Zealand Ministry of Justice.

Vaughan, B. (2000) 'Breaking out of jail: Generating non-custodial penalties for juveniles', *Irish Criminal Law Journal*, vol 10, pp 14–18.

von Hirsch, A. (1985) *Past or future crimes: Deservedness and dangerousness in the sentencing of criminals*, New Brunswick: Rutgers University Press.

von Hirsch, A. and Roberts, J.V. (2004) 'Legislating sentencing principles: The provisions of the Criminal Justice Act 2003 relating to sentencing purposes and the role of previous convictions', *Criminal Law Review*, August, pp 639–52.

Walmsley, R. (2003) 'Global incarceration and prison trends', *Focus on Crime and Society*, vol 3, pp 65–78.

Walmsley, R. (2007) *World prison population list* (7th edn), London: King's College, International Centre for Prison Studies.

8

Where now?

Rod Morgan

Introduction and Setting

The seminar at King's which resulted in this volume was organised to stimulate thinking about the propositions put forward in Lord Carter's review, *Securing the future* (Carter, 2007). Consideration focused on two key recommendations:

- that a more structured sentencing framework be developed by establishing a permanent sentencing commission; that this proposition early be explored by a working group to consider its advantages, disadvantages and operational feasibility; with the working group reporting to the Lord Chancellor and Lord Chief Justice by summer 2008 (Carter, 2007, p 35);
- in order that the Government be able to cope with current prisons undercapacity that a range of measures be taken urgently to increase prison capacity and reduce the demands made on it; in addition to existing plans, there should be built three very large, multi-functional prisons, ineptly named Titans, each providing 2500 additional prison places. (Carter, 2007, p 38)

These two proposals had by early May 2008 gained considerable momentum. In relation to the first, the Lord Chancellor and Lord Chief Justice almost immediately, in January 2008, established a Working Group under the chairmanship of Lord Justice Gage. In late April the Gage Working Group, several of whose members participated in the seminar, published a consultation paper (Sentencing Commission Working Group, 2008) setting out a number of questions on which the Group sought opinion by 2 June 2008 with a view, as Carter recommended, that the Group reach conclusions and report to the Lord Chancellor and Lord Chief Justice by summer 2008. This, we must assume, meant reporting within a few weeks of the Group's deadline for submissions. Meanwhile Ministry of Justice ministers announced that Titan prisons, or multi-functional prison clusters as they preferred to call them, were now part of the government's prison-building programme. Although the Lord Chancellor promised a consultation early in 2008 and subsequently in April, the consultation paper did not appear until 5 June. By the time the seminar took place, however, advertisements had appeared in the press for both suitable brownfield sites in the South East, the Midlands and the North West and the appointment of a senior manager to head up their selection and development.

The seminar was thus not merely timely, but during the course of the day it took on an air of urgency. Events were moving apace. If policy was to be influenced then those intent on exercising influence had no time to lose. Written submissions needed to be put in very soon indeed.

The participants at the seminar fell into three broad groups: a very few policy *insiders* from the Ministry of Justice or the Treasury; a few policy *insiders* or academic *outsiders*, who, for these particular policy purposes, were *co-opted insiders* (notably members of either the Gage Committee or the two precursors of any sentencing commission that might be established, namely the Sentencing Guidelines Council (SGC) and the Sentencing Advisory Panel (SAP)); and policy *outsiders* (namely academics, officers from penal pressure groups or research centres or practitioner field-staff – prison governors or chief officers of probation, etc). Among the latter group, the overwhelming majority, prior detailed knowledge of these policy developments varied a great deal. Some participants were very much aware and had read all the key documents. Others knew only sketchily of what was going on and used the day to get up to speed, a task in which the insiders, embedded or co-opted, were keen to assist.

It is not straightforward therefore to summarise the views of all the participants on the two major issues under discussion. We were not representative of any constituency and some of our number, by virtue of their roles and policy engagement, were understandably reticent about stating personal views despite the usual 'Chatham House Rules' assurances (namely, that no one would subsequently report who had said what). Outsiders, insofar as they felt sufficiently well informed either prior to the event or during the course of the day, were most forthcoming. But two dominant opinions, not however shared by everyone, began to emerge: first, that the idea of a sentencing commission should receive serious consideration and not be lost either because of short-term party political considerations or perceived judicial hostility; and second, that the construction of Titan prisons should ideally be avoided.

The proposed sentencing commission

No-one at the seminar quarrelled with Nicola Lacey's account (Lacey, 2008; see also Downes and Mayan, 2007) of the auction in toughness which has characterised English and Welsh party politics and penal policy in recent decades (Scotland and Northern Ireland have followed rather different courses). This auction is part of the neo-liberal market economy agenda to which both New Labour and the Conservative Party is now wedded. It has driven up the prison population to ever greater heights, which in May 2008 stood at a new record high of over 82,000. There was rather less agreement as to whether this penal bidding war had been profoundly damaging and costly for the polity and whether wise politicians might now be seeking a way out of what Lacey termed their 'prisoners' dilemma'. A sentencing commission – expert, dispassionate, independent and set at arm's length from the executive, led and probably dominated by the judiciary, the penal equivalent of the Monetary Policy Committee established by Gordon Brown when Chancellor of the Exchequer to set bank interest rates – offered, Lacey suggested, a way out of this prisoners' dilemma. It seems clear that ministers, past and present, *are* in a bind, to which some privately admit. The politicians' dilemma lies in the fact that the Treasury is not persuaded that expanding the prison population represents a sensible investment in terms of crime reduction and drives a hard bargain when extra funds are awarded. Analysis of Prison Service budgets for recent years shows that the unit cost of imprisonment has been driven down to what may be dangerous operational levels, not least in terms of order-maintenance and reconviction rates. The system stands on the edge of an operational precipice (emergency use of police cells, failures in prisoner programme delivery, an absence of defensible resettlement arrangements, frequent overcrowding transfers, deteriorating staff management relationships, etc) and is arguably unsustainable. This is the starting point for Carter's proposal that there be built Titan prisons. Further, any sign of 'law and order' weakness should any of the standard executive initiatives to reduce the prison population be taken is likely to be ruthlessly exploited by government critics. 'Soft on crime' or 'irresponsible failure to plan' is likely to be the *Daily Mail* and Opposition accusation. Therein lies the politicians' double bind.

Whether or not politicians might see advantage in the sentencing commission strategy as a way out of their front-line exposure was not something on which the seminar participants agreed. Some considered the prospect implausible. It was unlikely that ministers would give up the policy opportunity to suggest or introduce tougher sanctions in response to whatever latest horrendous crime event might occur: the electoral benefits of reserving such powers to themselves were too lucrative and proven. It was true that we now had a Prime Minister, Gordon Brown, who, unlike his predecessor, Tony Blair, did not have 'law and order' as one of his signature policies. Further, the Home Office had been separated from the Ministry of Justice with a New Labour elder statesman, Jack Straw, heading the latter. Moreover, in the youth justice field, the new Department for Children, Schools and Families under Ed Balls was challenging the omniscience of the Ministry of Justice. 'Law and order' party political power and influence, and its welfare alternatives, was now better spread within the government with less of the detail being driven from Number 10. The creation of a sentencing commission might spread responsibility, and thus government risk, even further. Yet Lacey confessed that the runes did not currently look favourable. Contrary to many commentators' expectations, Brown, she noted, appeared to be adopting a Blair-like 'law and order' strategy, going for broke with the proposal that the period of pre-trial detention without charge for terrorist suspects be increased from 28 to 42 days and pushing through Prison Service efficiency savings by locking up prisoners for longer at weekends in order to save money (Lacey, 2008, p 20).

Indeed the signs immediately prior to the King's College seminar looked even less auspicious and have since deteriorated further. Literally days before the local government elections in May 2008 Prime Minister Brown personally intervened to stop the announcement of a planned rise in prisoners' wages (*The Guardian*, 30 April 2008). The government nevertheless fared disastrously in those elections and two weeks later suffered a major defeat at the hands of the Conservatives in the

Crewe and Nantwich by-election. It seems highly unlikely that Gordon Brown and his government, wounded and struggling for survival, will, in the two years left before there has to be a general election, introduce a major and highly controversial policy such as the creation of a sentencing commission on the lines suggested by Carter.

However, some of those present at the seminar were not persuaded that it would be an advance *were* the government to adopt the Carter proposal. Would not the Gage Committee's interpretation of what was possible involve 'locking in' existing sentencing tariffs with little or no prospect of their being reduced? Carter had commented favourably on the benefits of the sentencing commission examples of Minnesota and North Carolina (Carter, 2007, p 32). But Gage had pronounced that US 'sentencing grids, particularly the way that account is taken of previous criminal history, is overly formulaic and mechanistic to an extent that is inimical to our tradition of judicial discretion' (Sentencing Commissioning Working Group, 2008, para 1.7). Unlike the US we do not have a codified system of criminal offences broken down into sub-categories according to seriousness. We have, for example, single offences of murder and robbery, the former covering such disparate acts as domestic mercy killings and lethal acts of terror and the latter covering everything from the armed hold-up of a post office to the taking by force of pocket money by one child from another in a school playground. Further, though there has been established the SGC and the SAP, and though the former will shortly have 'promulgated guidelines in respect of all the priority high volume, high custody offences', the SGC does not know what the consequences of its guidance are for the prison population nor has it the ability to monitor the degree to which its guidelines are followed (Gage, 2008, paras 2.17–2.25). This is the penal equivalent of deciding to fish with tackle devoid of knowledge of the fish inhabiting the water.

> The SGC can neither know the effect of its guidelines in terms of prison population before they are promulgated; nor does it have the means to predict what will be their effect. (Gage, 2008, para 2.25)

This Carter had fully recognised (Carter, 2007, paras 27–8). No doubt anticipating the opposition of the English judiciary to American-style sentencing guidelines, both he and the Gage Committee suggest that the starting point for the introduction of a more structured sentencing framework in England and Wales should be building on the work of the SGC and the SAP, possibly merged. This body would develop 'a single comprehensive set of indicative guideline ranges' covering 'sentence lengths, types of community sentences and the level of financial penalty, for groups of all offences, ranked by seriousness and offender characteristics' (Carter, 2007, para 30). This 'first version' would be derived 'from *current* sentencing practice' (Carter, 2007, para 31, emphasis added; see also Gage, 2008, para 6.1). Only when a structured, sentencing framework had been developed and the predictive capacity of that sentencing framework for the workloads of the probation and prison services been established would the government and the proposed English Sentencing Commission be able to tackle the question as to whether reliance on our use of imprisonment should be reduced and, if so, to what degree. Gage made clear that the degree to which overall sentencing practice should be tied to financial resources and limits placed on prisons' capacity was not an issue proper for the Working Group to discuss and it would not do so (Gage, 2008, para 1.6). Mike Hough, in his presentation, expressed the view that Carter had downplayed some of the key factors resulting in the growth in what he called 'penal greed' (see Jacobson, Roberts and Hough, this volume). For him, political problems need political solutions, and most participants agreed that scale of imprisonment was not a question for a sentencing commission to decide, any more than judicial decisions in individual cases should ever be made with regard to penal resource consequences, a point on which both Carter and Gage were emphatic (Carter, 2007, para 33; Gage, 2008, para 1.5(a)).

All of which meant, the more sceptical participants felt, that we were necessarily faced with the continuation of existing sentencing tariffs and practice for many years, with no guarantee that, when faced with the predictive data generated by a beefed-up SGC/SAP sentencing commission armed with comprehensive, structured guidelines, would there be any political will to ratchet back our reliance on custody. Indeed the opposite might well be the outcome. There were plenty of senior politicians on both sides of the political divide arguing that our prison population was not particularly high given the English serious crime rate, and at the most recent general election the Labour Party manifesto had boasted of the additional prison places that the government had provided (Labour Party, 2005, p 3). Some thought that Lord Carter, a New Labour 'fixer', had missed a valuable consultation opportunity by not engaging with the Opposition political parties before publishing his proposals. Possibly as a consequence of this lack of consultation both the Conservative and Liberal Democrat parties had spurned the government's invitation to have their nominated representatives on the Gage Working Party. All of which meant that, despite Nicola Lacey correctly arguing that our politicians' 'prisoners' dilemma' is not a true 'prisoners' dilemma' because they are able to talk to each other and reach a rational and consensual policy solution (Lacey, 2008, p 18), they weren't talking. Indeed the Conservative Party, that most likely to win power from Gordon Brown by summer 2010, had already rejected the idea of a sentencing commission.

What alternative way forward was offered by the sceptics, however? None emerged. And, given the widespread agreement that any sensible crime control policy must include scaling back our use of custody and shifting the centre of penal expenditure gravity towards the community, two plausible alternative policy strategies came to mind. First, muddling through the prisons crisis by using one or another of the many executive release mechanisms as and when necessary (for a comprehensive review of these mechanisms, see Tonry, 2003). Second, and a version of the former, reintroducing, possibly on the lines of the former borstal system, a systematic scheme of prisoner incentives for sentence compliance involving early release and community supervision. The former constitutes stop–go penal policy, is unjust, and generates cynicism about sentencing among sentencers and the public alike: the approach is inimical to public confidence in the criminal justice system and its legitimacy. The latter might ideologically appeal to the Conservative Party, but history suggests that all such partially indeterminate incentive systems are gradually corrupted by managerial considerations (for a history of the borstal system, for example, see Hood, 1965) as well as being vulnerable to prisoner manipulation.

Like the majority of the seminar participants, therefore, I was persuaded that taking forward, as described above, the sentencing commission proposal by building on the SGC/SAP framework already in place is the only potentially progressive policy approach available. I share the sceptics' fear that it may achieve very little, other than provide a more secure basis for planning prison-building policy. I also fear that the mechanism may be captured by political forces that will further drive up our reliance on imprisonment. But in the current neo-liberal, politics-of-fear environment, it is a proposal which should be supported. In the fag-end of Labour's third term it is not a proposal likely to be vigorously pursued. But we can hope that the responses to Gage are many and generally positive, that the government will ask Lord Justice Gage and his colleagues quietly to work up a detailed set of operational policy recommendations so that, given a more favourable political climate, there sits on the shelf a policy option ready to be given its head by a government willing to provide the leadership. It is this leadership in the realm of penal policy which we have so conspicuously lacked in recent years.

Titan prisons

Not much of a positive nature was said of Lord Carter at the seminar. He was regarded by many of the participants as a serial offender, the proposal that there be Titan prisons being only the latest in a line of what were regarded as seriously culpable recommendations (Carter, 2003, 2006, 2007). It is not true, however, that Carter was responsible for the policy fiasco that has been the creation of the National Offender Management Service (NOMS). Yes, he recommended that there be established a NOMS (Carter, 2003). But he provided only the very briefest sketch of what it might look like. It was the Home Office which immediately announced, without having worked out what the Service would operationally look like and what was feasible, that his recommendation be acted on (Home Office, 2004; for a general review of the NOMS saga see Hough et al, 2006). In fact Carter devoted the bulk of his 2003 report to sentencing, arguing that it had become increasingly punitive and setting out proposals for a reversal of that trend. About this the government did precious little – despite the fact that Carter argued that it was a precondition for the successful launch of a NOMS – which is why we have been brought to the present prison population crisis pass and Carter's emergency prison-building proposals.

Before considering the Titan proposals, Carol Hedderman reviewed the factors behind the rise in the prison population. What exactly was the nature of the prison population trend and was Carter's analysis and case for an emergency solution well founded?

Carter concluded that the current deficit in prison places, some 2–3,000 if normal operational margins are applied, would further increase during 2009 and, despite significant increases in capacity during 2010–11, would continue to grow, resulting in a potential deficit in excess of 8,000 places by the end of 2012. Ministry of Justice projections suggested this deficit would grow further to 10,500 by mid-2014 (Carter, 2007, para 8). Carter also argued that sentencing data currently collected 'do not contain sufficient detail to allow for meaningful analysis which can be acted on' as a result of which, and given the large number of other factors which can determine the size of the prison population, Ministry of Justice projections are revised at least once a year. It was precisely this failure of the projections to provide 'the predictability and consistency that would be useful when making policy, resource decisions and political judgements' (Carter, 2007, paras 14–15) that provided Carter with one rationale for establishing a sentencing commission.

There were some disagreements at the seminar about the nature of the prison population trend. Whether or not one agrees with Hedderman's critique of Carter's account of what is driving upwards prison numbers, these disagreements served to confirm Carter's assertions regarding the unreliability of Ministry of Justice projections. What is broadly clear is that the rise in the prison population has occurred not because more offenders have been brought to justice or that those who have been brought to justice have been more serious in character. The rise has been due principally (more than 80%) to sentences becoming progressively longer, with the rise in the recall and breach rate for community sentences making up most of the balance. The rise in sentence lengths has been greatest proportionately in the magistrates' courts, though those offenders sentenced in the lower courts account for only a small proportion of the average daily prison population. It is the apparently much smaller proportionate increase in the Crown Court which has had the greatest impact. Here, however, the waters have become muddy because indeterminate sentences for public protection (IPPs) are not included in the published average sentence length statistics and IPPs have been used to an extent significantly greater than forecast. There are already more than 11,000 indeterminate sentence prisoners in the prison population, a number set to grow further given the current absence of offending behaviour programme provision which might enable such offenders to demonstrate to the Parole Board that their risk of reoffending and harm is reduced. The result is a reduced release rate by the Parole Board.

Almost everyone at the seminar agreed that the public was not being better protected from reoffending by these trends, that the provision of additional prison places was a bad investment and would likely fuel further growth in the use of imprisonment rather than the reverse. Government leadership was once again called for. The public was not as punitive as was often asserted (Roberts and Hough, 2005). A more rational public debate about penal policy was required. Yet the pessimism about politicians taking a new direction in the light of their 'prisoners' dilemma' was not assuaged, the Titans were on the doorstep and the government, with no great enthusiasm, most participants considered, was shaking hands with them.

Alison Liebling's critique of Carter's 'efficiency-utilitarian' approach was broadly sympathised with but not everyone, perhaps least of all the prison practitioners, was persuaded, despite the assertions from the inspectorate of prisons, that the size of a prison, particularly if organised as a cluster of discrete units, need be as detrimental to good prison management, positive prisoner–staff relationships or effective resettlement outcomes as was claimed. Where was the comparative evidence regarding prisoner outcomes? None was advanced other than Hedderman's earlier evidence that, contrary to official statements, prisoner reconviction rates had not improved in recent years. What did become clear was that the government appeared already to be contemplating working with the private sector for developing Titan clusters and that a 'site masterplan' and project specification produced 'for consideration by Lord Carter's prison review team' contained disturbing elements. For example, one proposed 'low cost' site plan made provision for only one outdoor 90 x 80 metre football pitch for 2,500 prisoners and assumed crowding of up to 30% (a Certified Normal Accommodation of 2,000 with an operational capacity of 2,600), intensive building within the perimeter and an overall site, almost one third of which is was to be taken up with staff and visitor car parking space, of only 44 to 60 acres (Wates, 2007). If taken up, such project plans were generally considered disastrous. It was pointed out that, despite the early performance promise of commercially-managed prisons, all those currently in operation were in the lower half of the Prison Service's own performance table. Further, all the evidence indicated that most were not cheaper than their Prison Service-managed comparatives and had significantly higher staff turnover rates.

There was much reformist talk about the more effective regionalisation of prisons administration and governance, but no alternative clear way through the management of the prisons capacity deficit was identified. Muddling through, taking every conceivable measure marginally to increase capacity and reduce the demand made on the prison system, was favoured in preference to the Titan model, not least because, as was emphasised, despite all the talk of prison clusters, none were effectively in existence at present. Further, as Liebling emphasised, if Titans were not a suitable destination for women (Carter, 2007, para 21), what made them suitable for men?

Conclusion

The majority of the King's College seminar participants were galvanised by a pressing policy dilemma, the rising prison population driven principally by increasing sentence lengths rather than any proportionate increase in the use of imprisonment, and the proposition that in the short term this dilemma be resolved by building three so-called Titan prisons. Most persons present had little sympathy with the government. The prison population crisis had been both predictable and predicted: the government had largely failed to heed the warnings or plan accordingly. The proposed Titans represented a step away from a more progressive sentencing policy. They should be avoided at all costs. Yet the political climate was not conducive to a step forward.

The most that could be hoped for was that the case for a more structured sentencing framework be advanced in the hope that at some point in the future a Minister of Justice would use it as a vehicle to press for a reduced rate of imprisonment. I agreed.

References

Carter, P. (2003) *Managing offenders, reducing crime: A new approach*, London: Ministry of Justice.

Carter, P. (2006) *Legal aid: A market-based approach to reform*, London: Prime Minister's Strategy Unit.

Carter, P. (2007) *Securing the future: Proposals for the efficient and sustainable use of custody in England and Wales*, London: Ministry of Justice.

Downes, D. and Morgan, R. (2007) 'No turning back: The politics of law and order into the millennium', in M. Maguire, R. Morgan and R. Reiner (eds) *The Oxford handbook of criminology*, Oxford: Oxford University Press.

Hedderman, C. (2008) 'Building on sand: Why expanding the prison estate is not the way to "secure the future"' (this volume).

Home Office (2004) *Reducing crime, changing lives: The government's plans for transforming the management of offenders*, London: Home Office.

Hood, R. (1965) *Borstal re-assessed*, London: Heinemann.

Hough, M., Allen, R. and Padel, U. (eds) (2006) *Reshaping probation and prisons: The new offender management framework*, Bristol: The Policy Press.

Labour Party (2005) *Britain forward not back: The Labour Party manifesto 2005*, London: Labour Party.

Lacey, N. (2008) 'The prisoners' dilemma in England and Wales' (this volume).

Roberts, J.V. and Hough, M. (2005) *Understanding public attitudes to criminal justice*, Maidenhead: Open University Press.

Sentencing Commission Working Group (2008) *Consultation document*, London: Ministry of Justice.

Tonry, M. (2003) 'Reducing the prison population', in M. Tonry (ed) *Confronting crime: Crime control policy under New Labour*, Cullompton: Willan Publishing.

Wates (2007) *A 2,500-place prison for consideration by Lord Carter's Prison Review Team*, London: Ministry of Justice.

9

Endnote: latest developments in penal policy

Rob Allen

Following the King's seminar, a flurry of proposals has emerged about sentencing and imprisonment, some of which have been produced during a period of heightened political and media concern about crime, in particular violent crime involving knives. The most significant of these proposals in the long term relates to the development of the sentencing commission discussed in Chapter 4. It is important too that in July the Sentencing Advisory Panel (SAP) launched a consultation into the principles which guide the courts' decision making (SAP, 2008). Key questions include the circumstances in which custodial sentences should be imposed, what impact previous convictions should have on sentences, what weight should be given to all the different factors of an offence that might appear to make it more or less serious and whether the particular vulnerabilities of women offenders should have any impact on the approach to sentencing. The results of this consultation could exercise a profound impact on prison numbers and the prisons crisis. So too could a number of the other developments which have taken place between May and July 2008. The purpose of this endnote is to summarise these and assess the impact they might have on the future development of penal policy.

Growing criticism of Carter

The period since the seminar has seen growing criticism of the government's policy and the basis upon which it has been formulated. The House of Commons Justice Committee report, *Towards Effective Sentencing*, published on 22 July found Carter's review 'deeply unimpressive' and was concerned 'that this review was not evidence based and was a missed opportunity. It should have considered how to develop new ideas to address the problems with sentencing and provision of custodial and non-custodial facilities in England and Wales' (Justice Committee, 2008a).

A week earlier *The Times* newspaper published a letter from 10 leading parliamentarians, including former Conservative Home Secretary Lord Hurd, arguing that the decision to expand prison numbers was 'taken by the Government without debate or the publication of any supporting evidence that other options had been considered and rejected. No arguments were produced to suggest that such a large prison population will make England and Wales a safer place to live in' (*The Times*, 17 July 2008). July also saw the Rethinking Crime and Punishment initiative publish a manifesto based on the lessons from its seven years' work, which appeals to the government to invest the

£2.3 billion earmarked for building 'Titan' prisons in alternative punishments instead, including more intensive probation supervision, increased availability of restorative justice and improved dialogue between the providers of community supervision and sentencers. The manifesto argued that strengthening the infrastructure of community supervision could reduce the use of short terms of imprisonment as well as open up greater opportunities for courts safely to grant bail and the parole board to release prisoners serving long sentences (Rethinking Crime and Punishment, 2008). It suggested too that measures should be developed outside prison for groups of offenders who fare particularly badly – women, children and young people and the mentally ill – a theme also given prominence in the Justice Committee report.

Government policy

Despite this criticism, there has been little sign thus far that the government is minded to think again about the Carter package. In May, the Justice Secretary told the Justice Committee inquiry into Justice Reinvestment that 'we need more prison places, on any realistic analysis of demand, over the next ten years' (Justice Committee, 2008b). The long-awaited consultation paper about Titan prisons finally published in June was limited in terms of the questions it posed, clarifying that it had already accepted Lord Carter's recommendations, including Titan prisons, and wanted to hear from 'all who have views and experience which could help shape these establishments so that they best contribute within an end-to-end offender management system' (Ministry of Justice, 2008b, p 14). The limited scope of the questions did not prevent representatives from 34 criminal justice organisations, including the Prison Officers Association, marking the close of the consultation by signing an open letter urging the Lord Chancellor 'to abandon these misguided proposals for Titan prisons before they come a reality' (*The Guardian*, letters, 28 August 2008). Notwithstanding its overarching commitment to the Carter agenda, in four policy areas the government has encouraged alternative ways forward which might serve to reduce demand for prison places.

First it has sought to promote community sentences as an alternative to short prison sentences, with the report *Community sentencing: Reducing re-offending, changing lives* arguing that: 'For serious, violent and persistent offenders, a long period behind bars is without doubt the right course of action. But for those who might otherwise receive a short prison term the evidence is clear – a community sentence can be more effective in terms of turning them away from crime' (Ministry of Justice, 2008a). A £40 million funding initiative has been launched to strengthen high-end community sentences in order to increase their viability as alternatives to prison.

Prisoners serving short sentences only comprise a small proportion of the daily prison population – those serving 12 months or under representing about 12.6% of the sentenced population. Yet even in respect of this group the Ministry of Justice's efforts to boost public and sentencers' confidence in alternatives have run into difficulties.

The report of a Cabinet Office Crime and Communities review undertaken by Louise Casey recommended that unpaid work should be more visible and demanding and that consideration should be given to contracting its delivery out from the Probation Service (Cabinet Office, 2008).

The second policy area in which positive developments are possible relates to women offenders. The Corston Review, accepted by the government, recommended that the majority of women held on short sentences or held on remand should not be sentenced to custody in most circumstances (Home Office, 2007). The report also suggested that fewer women should be returned to custody as a result of breaching their licence or community supervision. A snapshot of the female prison population in February 2008 (published in June in the government's six-monthly progress report on its response to Corston), showed that there were 4,389 adult women held in custody. Of these, 877 (20%) were being held on remand, spending on average 4–6 weeks in custody, with nearly 60% remanded in custody not going on to receive a custodial sentence. A further 789 (18%) were held on sentences less than 12 months. Some 193 of those sentenced from January 2008 onward were being held as a result of breaching their licence conditions. The data reveals a picture of a largely short-term female prison population, for whom there could be substantial scope for diversion from custody. The National Service Framework for Women Offenders launched on 30 May 2008 and a promised range of guidance on pre-sentence reports and liaison with sentencers are intended to exploit the potential for reducing the number of women in prison.

The third area of possible reform is in respect of juvenile offenders under 18, of whom there were 2,432 in prison at the end of May (plus a further 450 in other forms of secure accommodation). The run-up to the publication of the Youth Crime Action plan saw media speculation about a radical approach to the use of custody for this age group with the suggestions that responsibility for the detention might be removed from the prison service altogether (as was recommended by the Chief Inspector of Prisons as far back as 1996) or that local authorities might be required to pay for the costs of young people sentenced to custody – a measure which could help to drive down numbers (Allen, 2008). In the event, the Action Plan contains more modest proposals, setting out principles for the use of custody and promising to consult with local authorities about how to ensure that they take greater responsibility for reducing the number of young people who are locked up. Specific consultations are promised about whether local authorities should meet the full cost of court-ordered secure remands which would help them 'make the case for investment locally in alternative forms of remand such as use of fostering'. As for sentencing, the Plan commits only to making the costs of custody more visible in order to 'demonstrate the savings that are made where local areas reduce the use of custody and conversely the costs incurred when custody use increases'. The question of whether local authorities should be responsible for custodial placements and their funding is a matter of long-term debate (HM Government, 2008).

The fourth area of possible development relates to mentally disordered offenders. An independent review is underway, led by former Home Office minister Lord Bradley, which is examining the extent to which offenders with mental health problems or learning disabilities could, in appropriate cases, be diverted from prison to other services. The review was due to report in the summer but had not been published at the time of writing.

The climate

The climate of press and political opinion during the summer of 2008 has continued to exercise upward pressure on imprisonment. A series of deaths of young people by stabbing (including four in one day) has led to increased demands for a tougher approach.

The Sun newspaper started a campaign for the automatic prosecution of young people caught in possession of a knife, a measure which the government introduced in part in June with a policy that all over-16s found carrying a knife 'can expect to be prosecuted' with a similar expectation for those under 16 for a second offence. The *News of the World* Save Our Streets Campaign went much further, launching a petition demanding a minimum sentence of two years for carrying a knife without lawful reason; an end to automatic early release for anyone convicted of violent crime; and investment in a 10-year plan to build more prisons.

Although the government resisted calls from the Conservative Party for a mandatory custodial sentence, the Court of Appeal made it clear that carrying an offensive weapon including a knife should be dealt with more severely than hitherto given the 'current level of prevalence on a national scale' (*R v Povey, McGeary, Pownall and Bleazard* [2008] EWCA Crim 1262 (date of judgement: 21 May 2008). The Court asserted that 'offences of this kind have escalated and are reaching epidemic proportions ... and that in the public interest this crime must be confronted and stopped'.

Because 'conditions now are much more grave than they were', the Court ruled that guidance from the Sentencing Guidelines Council to magistrates should normally be applied at the most severe end of the appropriate range of sentences.

Offences related to carrying a knife are not the only ones which are likely to see an escalation in penalties. Further pressure on the prison system is likely to result from the Sentencing Guideline Council guideline on driving offences resulting in death; and the government review of the Bail Act in cases of murder could also lead to more use of pre-trial detention in these cases.

Conclusion

Over the last 15 years in England and Wales prison numbers have risen more sharply than almost any other comparable country (New Zealand is the exception). On top of this the government has decided to expand the capacity of the prison system by a further 15% with the Conservatives pledging to match that and more should they form the next administration.

This planned expansion has been based on almost no informed public debate. Lord Ramsbotham called in June for a standing royal commission on prisons and the House of Commons Justice Committee is holding an inquiry into the effectiveness of spending on criminal justice more widely. But Lord Carter's review, *Securing the future*, on which government has based its policy looked very narrowly at the issue of supply of and demand for prison places. More fundamental consideration of the proper use of imprisonment and alternatives and their relation to broader questions of social policy was beyond its remit.

There has been nothing in England and Wales remotely along the lines of the Scottish Prison Commission, which recommended cutting Scotland's prison population by a third. This is surprising given that, as a Conservative front bencher said in a debate on sentencing in the same month, 'the rise in the number of prisoners from 60,000 to 83,000 should not be a point of pride. It should be a point of shame.'

And it represents a major turnaround in the government's policy from 2002 when the White Paper *Justice for all* listed the then record prison population of 71,000 as one of the elements that was not working and pledged that radical reforms would ensure that prison was reserved for those who could not be dealt with in any other way (Home Office, 2002)

Since then, the government appears to have developed a different policy which credits prison with a positive impact. Jack Straw told the Justice Committee in May that:

Although the link is imprecise, there is some linkage between the fact that crime, as measured by the British Crime Survey, has dropped by a third in the last 11 years and the prison population has gone up by a third, and it is not a direct linkage, but I am not in any doubt that it is there and the fact that prison terms have got longer is also a factor' (Justice Committee, 2008b). Even the document designed to promote alternatives opens with the sentence: 'Prison works, but it's not the answer for all offenders.'

The questions raised by the contributions at the King's seminar and the issues to arise in the three months after it took place together make a strong argument for a fuller and more independent inquiry into the way forward in penal policy. As the Justice Committee has said:

Building new prisons will not solve the fundamental and long-term issues that need to be addressed in order to manage the escalating prison population and move towards an effective sentencing strategy. Moreover, this approach was initiated without sufficient investigation into the costs and benefits and in spite of the Government's own statements that the provision of new places does not present a long-term solution to the current prison crisis. (Justice Committee, 2008a)

References

Allen, R. (2008) 'The costs of custody', in M. Blyth, R. Newman and C. Wright (eds) *Children and young people in custody: Managing the risk*, Bristol: The Policy Press.

Cabinet Office (2008) *Engaging communities in fighting crime*, London: Cabinet Office.

Carter, P. (2007) *Securing the future: Proposals for the efficient and sustainable use of custody in England and Wales*, London: Ministry of Justice.

HM Government (2008) *Youth crime action plan*, London: Home Office.

Home Office (2002) *Justice for all*, Cm 5563, London: The Stationery Office.

Home Office (2007) *A report by Baroness Jean Corston of a review of women with particular vulnerabilities in the criminal justice system*, London: Home Office.

Hurd, D. et al 'A rational debate about new prisons', *The Times*, 17 July 2008.

Justice Committee (2008a) *Towards effective sentencing*, London: Stationery Office.

Justice Committee (2008b) Evidence, 13 May, www.publications.parliament.uk/pa/cm200708/cmselect/cmjust/uc425-ii/uc42501.htm

Ministry of Justice (2008a) *Community sentencing: Reducing re-offending, changing lives*, London: Ministry of Justice.

Ministry of Justice (2008b) *Consultation Paper CP10/08 Titan Prisons*.

Rethinking Crime and Punishment (2008) *The manifesto*, London: Esmée Fairbairn Foundation.

Sentencing Advisory Panel (2008) *Consultation paper on overarching principles of sentencing*, London: Sentencing Guidelines Council.